The Method of Shared Concern

A positive approach to bullying in schools

Ken Rigby

ACER Press

First published 2011
by ACER Press, an imprint of
Australian Council *for* Educational Research Ltd
19 Prospect Hill Road, Camberwell
Victoria, 3124, Australia

www.acerpress.com.au

sales@acer.edu.au

Edited by Rosemary Barry
Cover and text design by ACER Project Publishing
Cover art by Allan Addams
Typeset by ACER Project Publishing
Printed in Australia by BPA Print Group

National Library of Australia Cataloguing-in-Publication data:

Author:	Rigby, Ken.
Title:	The method of shared concern: a positive approach to bullying in schools / Ken Rigby.
Edition:	1st ed.
ISBN:	9781742860077 (pbk.)
Notes:	Includes bibliographical references and index.
Subjects:	Bullying in schools – Australia. School discipline – Australia.
Dewey Number:	371.58

This book is printed on Master Laser Paper derived from well-managed forests and other controlled sources certified against Forest Stewardship Council® standards, a non-profit organisation devoted to encouraging the responsible management of the world's forests.

Foreword

Before Ken Rigby made his decision to cultivate the Method of Shared Concern, he carefully studied the main approaches in the field of anti-bullying. He published his results in *Bullying interventions in schools: Six basic approaches* (Rigby, 2010b). But why did he choose this method?

The first clue appears if we observe that he describes how it is used with *suspected* bullies.

Why?

There is a big advantage in dealing with them as if they are just suspected. This avoids investigating their guilt. You can then concentrate on finding the clues leading to the miracle of a shared solution.

A thinking reader, reading Ken Rigby's know-how, will discover in his or her practice that this mindset will bring about reliable results.

Anatol Pikas
Uppsala, Sweden, 2010

Contents

Appendices

Tables

Figures

To Anatol Pikas, the originator of the Shared Concern Method, a thinker of genius who saw further than anyone else how bullying could best be overcome

Quotes from the experts

American educators would be wise to have this book handy when dealing with cases of school bullying. The Method of Shared Concern *is a positive strategy for handling incidents of school bullying, one less familiar to American educators. Dr. Rigby's book provides detailed information about how and when to apply this approach; his style is very engaging and his expertise is evident. Dr. Rigby provides a step-by-step guide to using the method, and also helps educators provide a rationale for adopting this effective strategy, and information about professional development. That is, this volume provides everything a busy educator needs to make a difference in how bullying is handled. My recommendation? This book should be required reading for American educators.*

Sheri Bauman, Associate Professor,
Director, School Counseling Program,
University of Arizona, USA

When what we do is not achieving our goals why do we persist doing the same thing? In his latest book Dr. Rigby provides schools with well informed evidence-based strategies and information about effectively addressing bullying with a particular focus on bullying involving a group. This book will change our thinking and the actions we take. An essential read for every school leader, Wellbeing Coordinator and anyone who wishes to prevent and successfully address bullying.

Jacqueline Van Velsen,
Wellbeing/Youth Services,
Catholic Education Office, Ballarat Diocese, Australia

The Method of Shared Concern is both a rational approach and an intuitive one. Dr. Pikas sensed that what most so-called 'bullies' are missing in their lives is the presence of a safe and caring adult. The fact that the adult approaches the members of the bully group in a non-judgmental manner, over a period of time, is a great help to these children who are caught in the bully dynamic. The adult continues to regularly and gently develop this caring relationship with exactly those young people who need it the most (and receive it the least, as they usually avoid relationships with adults, preferring to be with their equally immature peers). Under the guidance of an adult, who is not afraid to quietly and empathetically take charge, these 'bullies' can start to lean on and take guidance from someone who can see the bigger picture. Dr. Rigby's book makes the Method of Shared Concern easy to understand and apply. I will continue to encourage the schools, here in Quebec and also in the rest of Canada, to embrace the Method of Shared Concern, as it is one of the most developmentally sound ways of intervening in the bully dynamic. Dr. Rigby's book will be a great help in this journey.

Eva De Gosztonyi, Psychologist and Coordinator,
The Centre of Excellence for Behaviour Management, Montreal,
and faculty member, Neufeld Institute, Vancouver, BC, Canada

Preface

The purpose of this book is to explain the ideas underlying the Method of Shared Concern and show how they can be used in dealing with cases of bullying in schools. The basic ideas were first put forward by the Swedish psychologist Anatol Pikas. I have sought to develop them further for use in schools.

My familiarity with schools derives largely from my own experience as a schoolteacher over a 10-year period in both primary and secondary schools in England and Australia, and from visits between 1990 and 2010 to hundreds of schools in many parts of Australia where I act as an educational consultant. Conscious of the newness and radical nature of the Method, I have taken pains in this book to help teachers appreciate its qualities in comparison with alternative approaches with which they are often more familiar. In particular, I want schools to understand what they need to do if they decide to adopt the Method of Shared Concern.

The original ideas of Anatol Pikas provided the inspiration for this book. I was therefore delighted when he emailed me after reading the draft of the book to say: 'I am ready to state publicly that Ken Rigby is the person in the scientific community of research into bullying who has best understood my Shared Concern Method.'

It is nevertheless true that I have deviated in some ways from the practice he has suggested in his writing and workshops. I have accordingly called the method the 'Method of Shared Concern' to distinguish it from the earlier Pikas version known as the 'Shared Concern Method' (shades here perhaps of the 1979 Terry Jones movie *Life of Brian*, with its schism between the Judean People's Front and the People's Front of Judea). Still, I believe that the distinction is worth making – and Pikas agrees.

I have been greatly encouraged also by the results of a recent Australian study undertaken by Coosje Griffiths and myself evaluating the effectiveness of the present version of the method (Rigby & Griffiths, 2010), funded and supported in 2010 by the Australian Department of Education, Employment and Workplace Relations (DEEWR). As described and examined in this book, applications of the method in four Australian states have been overwhelmingly successful, leading to its endorsement by the then minister for education, Julia Gillard (currently prime minister), and its growing acceptance in Australian schools.

Outside Australia it is clear that the method, or versions of the method, are now being employed in a variety of countries including Sweden, England, Scotland, Canada, the United States, Spain, Germany, Estonia, New Zealand, Malaysia and Finland. There are also substantial numbers of practitioners of the method from around the world who have agreed to be included in this book as advisers in its use in schools. Their readiness to help is greatly appreciated. It gives me great hope that the problem of school bullying will ultimately be solved.

Ken Rigby
October, 2010

Acknowledgements

First and foremost, my thanks go to the gifted originator of the Shared Concern Method, the Swedish psychologist Anatol Pikas. Without his inspiration this book could not have been written. He should, however, be in no way held accountable for any shortcomings, misjudgements or mistakes in what I have written. I have, on his advice, called my contribution the Method of Shared Concern to distinguish my own interpretation from his. I am happy to do so. Each of us must act according to his own lights. But let me add this. More than any other individual, Anatol Pikas has illuminated the field of bullying interventions. In my own way, I have earnestly sought to tell others about the path that he has asked us to follow.

Second, I would like to thank the many colleagues and co-workers who have helped me enormously to gain a better grasp of how the method works in practice. This was made possible first by the Australian Department of Employment, Education and Workplace Relations, who provided a grant to undertake an evaluation of the use of the method in Australian schools. In this I was greatly assisted by Ms Coosje Griffiths and Ms Tracey Weatherilt, both of the Education Department of Western Australia. Together Coosje and I planned and carried out a study of the implementation of the method in schools in South Australia, Western Australia, Tasmania and Victoria. In evaluating the method we were assisted by many teachers and counsellors in both state and private schools. Their contribution to a deeper understanding and informed appreciation of the Method of Shared Concern was invaluable.

Third, I have learnt a great deal from watching skilled practitioners of the method at work. These include Anatol Pikas, whose work I have observed closely in two workshops in Australia, and two Australian practitioners, Mr Bill Bates from the South Australian Police and Ms Kerry Jarvis, at the time student counsellor at the St Thomas More College in Adelaide. Their exemplary modelling of interventions using the method has been faithfully recorded in a DVD made by Readymade Productions under the direction of Mr Chris Faul.

Fourth, there is nothing like workshopping ideas and practices with teachers and counsellors to enable one to explore the strengths and limitations of a method they are being asked to use in the everyday hurly-burly of educating children in schools. I have been fortunate in being able to take advantage of numerous opportunities to run workshops on the Method of Shared Concern with practising school staff, mainly in Australia but also in Singapore, Malaysia and the United States. In particular, I am much indebted to Ms Jacqueline Van Velsen, youth services education officer with the Catholic Education Office in Ballarat, Victoria, whose support for education and training in the use of the method has been unwavering. In South Australia the work has been strongly supported and facilitated by Mr Greg Cox, a policy adviser in student behaviour management with the South Australian Department of Education and Children's Services, and Mary Carmody, senior education adviser with Catholic Education in South Australia. In Queensland and Victoria opportunities have been provided by the state education departments for me to work with schools in exploring their application of intervention methods. I have also been much enlightened over the years through working with Dr Sheri Bauman from the University of Arizona in examining how teachers and counsellors around the world believe they can best tackle cases of school bullying. I am also indebted to Canadian psychologist Eva de Gosztonyi for her helpful advice on the use of the method, and her understanding based on her experience of its application in Canada.

My thanks also go to the School of Education at the University of South Australia for providing me with assistance in my role as Adjunct Professor to complete this work, and to the Hawke Research Institute, with which I am currently affiliated.

Thanks to Allan Addams, who provided the cartoons that appear as figures 3, 6, 7, 8, 9, 10 and 11 (see www.cartoonguy.com.au); to fotosearch, for permission to use the illustration that appears as figure 2 (www.fotosearch.com/photos-images/bully.html); and to Chris Achilleos, for permission to use the illustration of the dragon that appears on page xvii (www.chrisachilleos.co.uk).

Finally, thanks are due to the ACER staff with whom I worked, in particular Debbie Lee and Yana Gotmaker, and to my editor, Rosemary Barry, for their helpful and patient work in producing this book.

Introduction

If you want to help someone who is having a hard time, try sharing your concern about that person with someone who can assist. Perhaps they will. This is the simple idea underlying an approach called the Method of Shared Concern.

Every day there are countless examples of its application. It is the primary way in which help is provided for the less fortunate. These include refugees, victims of natural disasters (earthquakes, tsunamis, typhoons, floods, forest fires, drought), people living in poverty, victims of domestic violence, the mentally and physically disabled, the old, victims of crime and persecution, and even endangered species such as seals and whales.

In each case it is believed that if we share our concern with the 'right people' there is a good chance that they will help in a practical way, commonly through an organised charity. Experience shows that the method works. Literally millions of dollars are collected for all manner of causes to provide help for those about whom concern has been raised. It manifestly works, provided that the sharing of concern is sincere and credible. There is nothing new or surprising about this.

In recent years concern has been raised about people who are repeatedly victimised by their peers. These are individuals who, for one reason or another, are unable to defend themselves adequately and find themselves in the company of individuals or groups who want to bully them, and are able to do so. They are given a hard time – sometimes catastrophically hard, such that their health and wellbeing are seriously undermined. Over the last 20 years numerous books and other publications have drawn attention to the plight of these people, and many suggestions have been made about how they can be helped.[1]

Many of these quite reasonably point out that we must work towards providing a social environment in which nobody wants to bully anyone. The emphasis must be placed upon more and better education promoting positive interpersonal relationships. And, in fact, a great deal is now being done in many schools to encourage students to behave respectfully and cooperatively towards each other. In addition, efforts have been made to deal more effectively with any cases of bullying that do arise, notwithstanding the proactive steps that the school may have taken to reduce the likelihood of bullying taking place. Some schools have called for a 'zero tolerance' approach, which is often interpreted to mean the employment of tough traditional disciplinary means to deter those who would otherwise engage in bullying their peers.[2] Others have proposed and employed less punitive means, such as mediation and restorative practices.[3] Despite these actions, however, the level of bullying remains unacceptably high in all countries, and largely undiminished.[4]

When we look at the evidence regarding the effectiveness of school-directed interventions to deal with *actual* cases of bullying, the news is far from encouraging. For instance, a great deal of bullying goes on without the school knowing about it. This is despite frequent exhortations from teachers for students to inform the school authorities if they or any other students are being bullied. According to research drawing upon student reports, only about 30 per cent of students who have been bullied have ever told a teacher about it. About half of these students reported that the situation did not improve after they had told a teacher; some 10 per cent reported that the situation got worse.[5] These are very revealing findings. It is accepted that students are the best judges of teacher effectiveness in intervening in cases of bullying. We must face the fact that currently, even when cases of bullying are identified, school staff commonly fail to help those who come to them for help.

This is not to blame the teachers. It is hard to stop cases of bullying from continuing. There are many other pressing problems that need their attention. But the number one reason why they are so often unsuccessful is that they are applying methods of intervention that are inappropriate and do not work.

The most frequently proposed method of helping victims of bullying, especially those being victimised by their peers, has been to identify and take disciplinary action against the perpetrators, the bullies.[6] The rationale for doing so is that punishment, or the threat of punishment, will deter the bullies and make the victims safer. The evident failure of this time-honoured approach has led many educators to consider alternative methods of intervention when cases of bullying come to light. Among these is the Method of Shared Concern.

The novelty of sharing concern in addressing cases of bullying

As we have seen, the idea of sharing our concern about those who are having a hard time, with a view to getting help for them, is widely accepted and widely employed – as long as the concern is expressed to people who can be expected to help the victims. The novelty of the Method of Shared Concern as it applies to school bullying is that it proposes that concern for the victim be *shared with the bullies.*

This idea, originating in the work of the Swedish psychologist Anatol Pikas[7], has been greeted in some areas with considerable scepticism, even derision. Extreme reaction was shown in public responses to the release of an Australian government-funded report by Rigby and Griffiths evaluating the Method of Shared Concern in 2010.[8] The method was described by some critics as unbelievably crazy, destined to make an increasingly serious problem immeasurably worse. Some opined that the only way to deal with bullies was through the infliction of physical pain. Several thought that we should bring back the cane.

Those who saw it as in some way enlightened were in a minority. Fortunately these included the then Australian Minister for Education and Workplace Relations, Julia Gillard, who had released the report. She observed that though the method might appear counterintuitive, teachers should know about it. She explained:

> *I think our natural reaction, maybe my natural reaction, your reaction if we heard about a child being bullied would be, go to confront the children or child doing the bullying. But what this report makes [clear] quite powerfully is often that [it] can just make things worse for the child who is the victim of the bullying. So we the adults think we've sorted it out because someone's been told off but then the next day, the bullying is even worse.*[9]

Clearly a great deal of explanation is needed before the Method of Shared Concern will be understood and adopted as a method of treating bullying in schools. This is the task before us. This is what this book attempts to do.

Endnotes

1. Since the early 1990s, many excellent books have been written examining the nature of bullying in schools and how it can be countered, from Olweus (1993) to Jimerson, Swearer and Espelage (2010).
2. At one level, the notion of 'zero tolerance' is undeniably reasonable. No-one should turn a blind eye to bullying. Unfortunately the slogan is also a dog-whistling punitive message for those who want to feel supported in adopting a 'no-nonsense' approach to all cases of bullying.
3. A critical account of the six major methods of intervention in cases of bullying in school is provided in Rigby (2010b).
4. A recent survey of bullying prevalence in 27 countries in Europe and North America found that a third of the children in the overall sample reported occasional bullying or victimisation, and around one in 10 children reported chronic involvement in bullying. This is despite some reductions in reported levels of bullying in schools over the last 10 years (Molcho et al., 2009).
5. These results, reported for a large sample of Australian students by Rigby and Barnes (2002), were similar to those provided by Smith and Shu (2000) in England.
6. Recent surveys conducted in a range of countries including the United States, Canada, Australia, Norway, Finland and Germany have shown that approximately three out of four teachers or counsellors would opt to use the traditional disciplinary approach in addressing cases of even relatively mild bullying (Bauman, Rigby & Hoppa, 2008; Rigby & Bauman, 2007, 2009).
7. The basic thinking underpinning the Method of Shared Concern as described in this book was derived largely from the work of Anatol Pikas (1989a; 1989b; 2002). His version was known as the Shared Concern Method.
8. An Australian report evaluating the Method of Shared Concern was released by the Department of Education and Workplace Relations in January, 2010. See Rigby and Griffiths (2010); available at <http://www.deewr.gov.au/Schooling/NationalSafeSchools/Documents/covertBullyReports/methodOFSharedConcern.pdf>.
9. From a transcript of a radio interview of Julia Gillard by Alan Jones on 2GB, 20 January 2010, accessed at <http://www.australia.to/2010/index.php?option=com_content&view=article&id=591:julia-gillard-hits-the-airwaves&catid=111:people>.

It must be very trying, just when you are going to do something noble and heroic and impetuous, to hear a mild voice urging you to stop and think. You feel much as Saint George would have felt if, when he had couched his lance to dash upon his foe, some academic person, with spectacles and an umbrella, had held up a pleading hand and said 'Please – please – one moment! Don't you think you ought to wait till you have heard what the dragon's view is?'

Walter Murdoch (1947)

Part 1 | Bullying, bullies and victims

The Method of Shared Concern was conceived as a method of addressing cases of bullying in schools. We begin therefore in chapter 1 with an examination of what constitutes bullying behaviour. Next, in chapter 2, we consider what is known about the kinds of individuals and groups who become involved in so-called bully/victim problems and, most importantly, the context in which interactions between those who are called 'bullies' and 'victims' take place.

Chapter 1 | Bullying

It is claimed that the Method of Shared Concern is an effective and appropriate way of dealing with cases of school bullying. We must therefore ask what we understand by the term 'bullying'.

Various definitions of bullying have been proposed. The most comprehensive is as follows:

> Bullying is the *systematic abuse of power* in interpersonal relations.

In unpacking this definition we might begin with the word 'abuse'. In using this term we are asserting that bullying involves acting wrongfully. We are acknowledging that bullying is morally unacceptable. There are ways in which power may be used appropriately, and there are ways in which it may be used inappropriately. In addressing bullying we must be clear about this distinction.

Second, we might focus on the word 'power' and consider what it denotes. One persuasive definition is that attributed to the English philosopher Bertrand Russell:

> *Power may be defined as the production of intended effects.*[1]

Bullying is conceived of as intentional behaviour – the perpetrator aims at using the power he or she possesses to bring about certain effects, such as the submission or humiliation of another person.

Importantly, power over people can only be exercised when there is an imbalance of power between the would-be perpetrator and the target. It is clearly not the possession of a given level of 'power' that is crucial, but rather the difference in power between those involved. We must be clear that for bullying to occur, there must be a power differential between the perpetrator and the target.

In practice, we find that the differential is rarely fixed. In the course of interpersonal interactions it may change. It may increase or decrease; there may even be a reversal so that the original perpetrator becomes the target.

We can of course point to what *appear* to be objective bases of power, such as greater physical power or strength; the power of numbers, evident when a group of people seek to coerce an individual; verbal power, as in the capacity to intimidate through the way one speaks; manipulative power, evident in the capacity to turn a situation to one's advantage; resource power, enabling one person to control others by providing or denying access to what they want or need; and status or social power, that can be used to overwhelm someone. Yet we know that in many cases being imposed on by such power depends upon a subjective element: that is, whether the target *allows* the imposition to take place. This is in no way blaming the victim or excusing the bully. When bullying occurs the fact is that the target believes – often with good reason – that adequately defending him or herself against the bullying is unrealistic.

Finally, our definition indicates that the action taken is 'systematic'. It is not something that is done on the spur of the moment. It is premeditated, planned. It is part of a strategy designed to bring about submission on the part of the target. Hence it is typically persistent and repeated. I emphasise *typically* because it is reasonable to say that bullying can occur on just one occasion – at a meeting, for example, or on a bus journey. The perpetrator nevertheless acts in a systematic way, thinking through what he or she is attempting to achieve and how it is to be done. The result may be such that the target needs support and, not unreasonably, fears that it will happen again.

The means of bullying

It is useful from time to time to review the many ways in which bullying can occur. It may therefore be helpful to consider the content of table 1, which seeks to classify and indicate some of the forms that school bullying may take.

Table 1 Some means of bullying, with examples

	Direct	Indirect
Verbal	Insulting language	Persuading another person to verbally abuse someone
	Name calling	Spreading malicious rumours
	Ridicule	Anonymous phone calls
	Cruel teasing or taunting	Offensive text messages and emails
		Posting hurtful content on website
Physical	Striking, kicking	Deliberately and unfairly excluding someone
	Spitting	
	'Happy slapping'*	Damaging pictorial or videoed content placed on a website
	Throwing objects	Removing or hiding possessions
	Using a weapon	
	Threatening gestures, such as repeatedly staring at someone	Repeatedly turning away

*'Happy slapping' involves staging a physical attack on someone, recording it and making the recording available to others, for instance through a website.

Bullying is also sometimes classified according to whether it constitutes racial/ethnic or sexual harassment. A further distinction may be made between traditional forms of bullying and cyberbullying, involving the use of electronic technology.

We are most familiar with overt forms of bullying, as in face-to-face verbal abuse and physical attacks. What is sometimes not acknowledged is that bullying may take covert forms, and that these can be equally harmful. There is also a tendency to consider forms of bullying in isolation, without recognising that children who are bullied are often subjected to different kinds of bullying, both overt and covert. A case in point is cyberbullying. Those involved in this practice are, generally speaking, also involved in traditional forms of bullying at school, as either bullies or victims.[2]

Individual and group bullying

We tend to think of bullying as what one person does to another in isolation. And, in fact, there are clear instances of bullying directed by one person towards another without anyone else being involved, and this can go on for a very long time. The victim may well accept the bullying (as long as it is relatively mild) as a condition of being in a relationship with another person, especially if it has some compensating positives. Or it may simply be that the victim is unable to avoid interacting with the bully.

Cases of bullying involving just two people may occur periodically when a more dominant person encounters someone he or she wishes to bully. Sometimes the perpetrator can be described as a 'serial bully', ever on the lookout for more and more vulnerable people who can be bullied. According to one researcher in Canada, approximately 40 per cent of students who engage in bullying have multiple victims.[3] Some of these serial bullies may operate alone, but many do so with the backing of a friendship group.

When victims are asked whether their tormentors consist of a group or are operating singly, they are somewhat more likely to say that they are bullied by a single individual, although many say that the bullying is sometimes done by a group and sometimes by an individual.[4] The part played by a group is not always evident to victims. Victims may not see that the bullying has actually taken place through the cooperation and/or influence of a group of students. The person delivering the insults or the blows may be acting *on behalf of* the group.

On some occasions, however, the role of the group is very obvious. Occasionally we may observe a mob of people directing their aggression towards a solitary individual. This kind of behaviour – sometimes called 'mobbing' – occurs from time to time, although it is relatively uncommon. It may take either a verbal or a physical form, or a combination of the two, as when someone is simultaneously jeered at and physically attacked by people. It may involve what has been called 'happy slapping'.[5] The 'mob' enjoys the spectacle of someone being humiliated, both during the predetermined assault and afterwards by watching a video recording of the incident that is posted on the internet.

More commonly, one or several members of a friendship group decide to bully someone they have selected for a verbal and/or physical attack. Their action is largely – if not entirely – determined by what they think will meet with the approval of the group to which they belong, or will gain the approval of the leader of the group. When the bullying takes place, other members of the group may or may not be physically present. They are nevertheless implicated and may bear some responsibility for what happens.

Often there are individuals present who may be described as bystanders. The term 'bystander' suggests 'standing by', or doing nothing. However, it is frequently applied to those who are present regardless of whether they act or not. If we take this more inclusive meaning of the word, we can identify bystanders fulfilling different roles: as assistants to the bully, as encouragers of the bullying, as defenders of the victim, and as passive observers. According to some Canadian research conducted in primary schools, bystanders in this sense are present 85 per cent of the time when bullying occurs in school playgrounds.[6] Bullying in schools can, to a large extent, be understood as the outcome of what the bystanders do in showing their approval or disapproval of what they see happening – or in just passively observing.

The prevalence of bullying

Numerous attempts have been made to estimate the prevalence of bullying in schools. For the most part, researchers have made use of anonymous questionnaires completed by students, parents and teachers.[7] Results from surveys suggest that about 50 per cent of students have experienced bullying at one time or another – usually relatively mild bullying. Estimates of the extent to which students are frequently bullied vary according to the age group sampled and the country where the study is conducted. It appears that between 9 and 15 per cent of students report being bullied weekly.[8] Some of these students experience intense and sustained bullying. These constitute a small minority; but, as is now well known, the harm can be considerable. The effects on the health of bullied children can be extremely serious and long lasting.

Not all forms of bullying are equally prevalent. Face-to-face verbal bullying is by far the most common among children of all ages. Physical bullying is more common among younger children. As students get older, overall bullying becomes less common, and the proportion of indirect to direct bullying increases. That is, in secondary schools there is proportionately more indirect bullying, such as exclusion, rumour-spreading and cyberbullying, than in primary schools.

Cyberbullying increased rapidly during the first decade of the twenty-first century as more and more people gained access to cybertechnology. Its prevalence in some countries now appears to have stabilised.[9]

The distribution of bullying according to severity

Understandably, concern about bullying tends to focus on the more extreme manifestations, such as repeated assaults and total exclusion. It is important, however, to recognise that most bullying is not so extreme. There is a temptation to ignore the less severe forms. This is mistaken. Low-level bullying in a school can be very hurtful to some students. Further, if the less severe forms can be successfully addressed the school ethos will change, and make it less likely that the more severe forms will occur.

The distribution of bullying according to severity is suggested in figure 1.

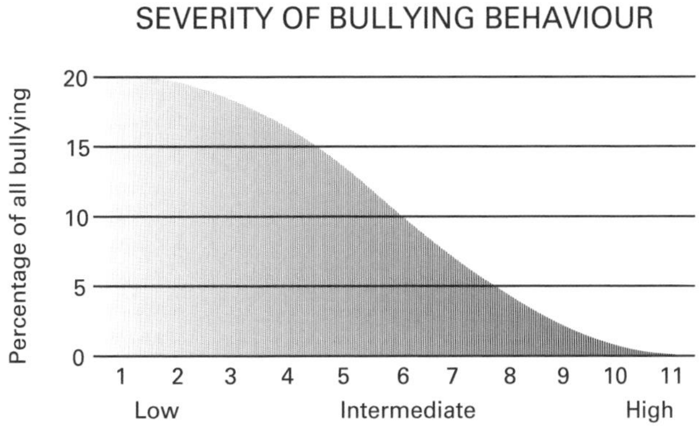

SEVERITY OF BULLYING BEHAVIOUR

Percentage of all bullying

20

15

10

5

0

1 2 3 4 5 6 7 8 9 10 11

Low Intermediate High

Figure 1 Continuum of bullying severity (Rigby, 2010b, p. 17)

Here are some suggestions that may be helpful in assessing the degree of severity or seriousness of different kinds of bullying behaviour[10]:

- **low severity**: commonly involves thoughtless periodic teasing, name-calling and occasional exclusion, and is regarded as annoying and unpleasant
- **intermediate severity**: the victim is subjected, for a time, to forms of harassment that are both systematic and hurtful, including cruel teasing, continual exclusion and some threats or relatively mild physical abuse, such as pushing or tripping

- **high severity**: the harassment is particularly cruel and intense, especially if it occurs over an extended period and is very distressing to the victim, frequently involving serious physical assaults but may still be severe when the bullying is non-physical as in total or almost total exclusion from groups.

In practice, assessing the severity of cases of bullying is not easy and a degree of subjectivity invariably enters into our judgements. We can be more confident of identifying extreme cases. Being repeatedly assaulted and isolated is recognised as more severe than occasionally being insensitively teased.

As well as taking into account the nature, frequency and duration of the bullying, a teacher may consider the hurt or harm that the victim has experienced. This latter consideration raises difficulties. Some students are more upset or react more strongly than others when they are bullied. Should we therefore take into account what the hypothetical 'average' student might feel? Or should our judgement be determined by how a targeted student is seen to be affected? There is no easy answer. Clearly no bullying should be ignored or trivialised. However, despite the acknowledged difficulties of making judgements of severity or seriousness, commonsense dictates that schools do so as a necessary step in assigning priorities in a school, and especially in choosing the most appropriate method of intervention.

The consequences of bullying

Much has been written about the consequences of bullying. It is now well established that low levels of both physical and psychological wellbeing are associated with being involved in bully/victim problems at school.[11] Longitudinal studies examining the extent to which students experience being bullied and changes in their mental and physical health strongly suggest a causal relationship. Those who are bullied most frequently at school are more likely to suffer a decline in wellbeing. Children who frequently engage in bullying others also tend to have relatively low levels of wellbeing; for instance, they are more likely than most students to experience depression and suicidal thinking.[12] It is clear that both perpetrators and victims of bullying need help; otherwise, they are likely to experience low levels of wellbeing, not only while they are at school but also later in life.[13] In examining the nature of bullying, we must keep in mind the two basic reasons why we should seek to stop it – it is wrong and it is harmful.

Is bullying normal?

From time to time I come across questionnaires that seek to assess knowledge of bullying. One of the questions sometimes asked is this:

Is bullying normal? Circle your answer

Yes No Don't know

The answer, we are generally told, is 'No.' But is this the case?

We can see why the 'correct' answer is 'no'. If bullying is normal it is acceptable; if it is acceptable we will do nothing about it. But there is another reason. We may *want* to think that the practice of bullying is not normal, that it is indeed unnatural; even (some say) evil, diabolical, something that must be severely condemned.

There are several lines of argument that may suggest that the right answer is actually 'yes'. One asserts that it follows from Darwinian theory – that humans as well as other organisms develop through a process of natural selection, crudely described at times as the 'survival of the fittest'. What is ignored in this argument is that humans can *decide* who is fit to survive: they can decide that they will include those people who cannot adequately defend themselves. And this is broadly what the best of civilisations have decided. This line of argument does not provide grounds for asserting that bullying is an inevitable – and therefore 'natural' – consequence of our evolutionary history.

A second argument is that bullying is normal in the sense that everybody, or nearly everybody, has at times an impulse towards hurting someone or putting someone under pressure. This can readily be confirmed by asking people whether they have ever felt like acting in this way. When I ask this question of students in anonymous questionnaires, a large majority say that they have. This is not the same thing as bullying, though it is an essential element in bullying behaviour. Depending on how you frame the question, most people will admit to trying to get their own back at one time or another by dominating somebody using means that are, to an outsider, patently unfair or excessive. If we interpret 'normal' as what most people at times think of doing, I think a case can be sustained for seeing bullying as 'normal'. We realise that the temptation to bully is hard to resist at times – and it is good to be aware of this.

Still we must – I think – concede that there are cases that can be reasonably described as 'unnatural'. These are cases of bullying involving extreme premeditated cruelty. One may think here of the James Bulger case in England.[14] The release after 11 years in prison of the boys who tortured and killed this two-year-old was understandably met with cries of anguish and demands that the killers should never be released. Statistically cases such as that of James Bulger, though indelibly imprinted on the public consciousness, are very rare. I think there must be very few people who can say that they have had an impulse to torture and kill an innocent child.

Saying that bullying is in a sense natural does not mean that we think it is desirable – far from it. What this statement does is recognise the human condition. This is apparent to anyone who picks up a history book. Read about the parade of both great and ordinary men and women who have from time to time abused their power, and it becomes hard to believe that bullying is always, or even mostly, 'unnatural'. At any rate the Method of Shared Concern accepts that we, as well as those we come to identify as bullies, have at times bullied others: that is we have ourselves abused our power.

The writer GK Chesterton responded to a newspaper invitation which asked its readers to say what they thought was wrong with the world. His simple reply was: I am.

This does not however mean that we should slacken our efforts to address bullying in children, any more than we should in ourselves.

Endnotes

1. Russell (1938), p. 23.
2. According to Smith et al. (2008), a large majority of students in England who reported being victims of cyberbullying were being bullied concurrently by 'traditional' means at school.
3. Sometimes as many as 15 (Chan, 2006).

4. A large-scale survey of over 30 000 Australian schoolchildren revealed that while most respondents who were bullied indicated that it was undertaken by one student, some 25 per cent indicated that a group of students was also involved (Rigby, 2002, p. 282).
5. 'Happy slapping' is a term used to describe the practice of physically attacking (originally, slapping) a person and filming the attack using a mobile phone. The recording may be sent to others or posted on websites for public viewing, to further humiliate the victim.
6. According to this research, no attempt was made by bystanders to stop the bullying in approximately 75 per cent of cases (Pepler & Craig, 1995).
7. Examples of such questionnaires are contained in a package known as the Peer Relations Assessment Questionnaires (PRAQ). The package includes questionnaires and instruction manuals suitable for use with senior students; junior students (using pictorial representations); teachers; and parents (see Rigby, 2010d). Other questionnaires may be found at <http://www.kenrigby.net>.
8. In the United States Nansel et al. (2001) found that 8.8 per cent of students in years 6–10 reported being bullied on a weekly basis. In a roughly comparable study in Australia, Rigby (1998a) estimated that approximately 15 per cent were being bullied weekly.
9. In a 2002 study in England among year 7 and 8 students, some 13 per cent reported receiving one or more nasty or threatening text or email messages; this rose to 16.4 per cent in 2004 before beginning to decline slightly in 2005–06 (see Rivers & Noret, 2009.) However, as new means of bullying through cybertechnology became available after 2006, for example through Facebook and smart phones, it is possible that such bullying has become more common.
10. Rigby (2002) pp. 41–42.
11. The effects of bullying on the mental and physical wellbeing of schoolchildren have been examined in numerous studies. For summaries of findings, see Rigby (2001, 2003).
12. The experience of bullying others at school has repeatedly been shown to be related to depression and suicidal ideation (see Rigby, 1998b, 1999; Rigby & Slee, 1999; Roland, 2002).
13. Longitudinal studies monitoring the mental health of students who have been severely bullied at school show that the effects can be long-lasting; for example, students who identified as victims of school bullying at the age of eight are about three times more likely than others to be excluded from National Service in Finland approximately 10 years later (Ronning et al, 2009).
14. James Bulger was a two-year-old child who was abducted, tortured and murdered by two older boys in Liverpool, England in 1993. The release of the two older boys produced an anticipated storm of protest (see <http://everything2.com/title/James+Bulger>).

Chapter 2 Bullies and victims

In tackling cases of bullying we invariably begin with some notion of what bullies and victims are like. We have certain pictures in our heads of these characters, and they help to determine how we will treat them when a bully/ victim problem comes to our attention.

Let us begin with a popular stereotype of the 'bully' as illustrated in figure 2.

Figure 2 The stereotypical bully and victim (©Art Parts)

This illustration fits the criteria defining bullying given in chapter 1. There is a clear imbalance of power, physical in this case. Power is evidently being abused. The target is being oppressed, indeed humiliated. One may surmise that the action is systematic. The bully is enjoying having an audience that he is seeking to impress.

But it would be unreasonable to suppose that this kind of bullying is typical. As we know, most bullying is verbal, and a good deal of bullying is covert and indirect.

There is a view that bullies can be readily identified through the personality characteristics they display. They are commonly seen as aggressive, bossy, unempathic, and insensitive towards others. If so, we should be able to pick bullies without knowing how they have actually behaved in the past. This was once put to the test. In my early years of inquiring into school bullying (around 1990) a colleague and I (both practising psychologists at the time) undertook a pilot inquiry at a primary school in South Australia. We asked teachers to send us, one by one, students for whom there was evidence that they had recently engaged in bullying their peers; students who had been recently victimised; and students who were not known to have been involved in any bullying. They were not to tell us beforehand to which category the students belonged. Our role was to chat with the students about school life without bringing up the subject of bullying. Subsequently it became clear that there was almost no correspondence between the judgements made by the teachers and those made by the two psychologists on the basis of their chats with the students.

Why had our efforts to identify bullies on the basis of their personalities as revealed in interviews proved to be generally unsuccessful? One reason was that the teachers had evidence of the students' actual behaviour when they interacted with their peers and we had not. Another was that our implicit theory of what bullies are like was misguided. We had expected to find students who were 'bullies' to give themselves away by their tough-minded, belligerent attitudes. We expected to find students who were prejudiced and insensitive, possibly disturbed. Subsequently we were informed that some students we had found to be amiable and good-natured were (according to teachers) among the worst bullies.

In the succeeding years there were to be numerous published studies of the correlates of children who bully others. Not surprisingly bullies do tend to be bigger and stronger than others, especially if they are boys.[1] They also tend to differ from others on some psychological dimensions. Many thousands of students have now completed questionnaires containing tests designed to measure such characteristics as extraversion, psychoticism, self-esteem, depression, empathy, narcissism and machiavellianism. Results from these tests have been correlated with results from reliable measures of bullying behaviour. Small though significant correlations have sometimes been reported. For example, children with elevated scores on measures of bullying have been found to be somewhat less empathic and more insensitive than others, and somewhat more manipulative.[2]

But these psychological characteristics account for comparatively little variation in bullying behaviour among students. To the surprise of some counsellors, most studies have found no relationship between level of self-esteem and bullying. As a means of identifying bullies, personality tests are clearly not very reliable. There is obviously far more to it than personality.

In seeking to generalise about the 'bully', we are assuming that all bullies are alike. Given that a very large proportion of people *sometimes* engage in bullying of various kinds – some relatively mild, some extremely severe, some as lone individuals, some with the support of groups – discovering a strong basis for bullying behaviour in the 'personality' is not likely to be successful. Students who constantly engage in bullying are a mixed bunch. Here is my attempt to categorise them.

The bully

The lone bully

Such a person does not appear to be influenced by those around. He or she is unconnected, or only very loosely connected, with any group of friends, and may be socially alienated. This person's bullying behaviour appears to be driven by a strong personal need to dominate others without any regard for what is fair or for the suffering of those who are bullied. Reinforcement from bystanders who observe what is happening may indeed be gratifying, but is not necessarily the driving force. The motivation appears to derive largely from personal abuse or neglect the person has experienced, commonly from parents, fuelling hostile feelings towards others in general.[3]

Among children who bully, such cases are in a minority.

The bully–victim

It is now widely acknowledged that classifying individuals as bullies, victims and others is highly simplistic and often misleading. Nobody is a bully or a victim all the time, and sometimes a person may not unreasonably be regarded as both a bully and a victim. In fact, a significant proportion of students who tend to engage in bullying quite frequently are also quite frequently bullied by others. It has been estimated that about 20 per cent of students who are classified as bullies are also victimised by others.[4]

These students are referred to as 'bully–victims.' In some cases they may have been motivated to bully others because they have themselves been bullied. However, as a rule, bullying others does not enable these students to feel secure. Unlike those who have been called 'pure bullies', their attempts to dominate others are often unsuccessful. One would expect this subgroup of bullies to have some of the characteristics of victims – for example in being somewhat mentally less stable and more depressed than average – and that is what has been found.[5]

The bully under the influence of peers

Individuals described as bullies often bully under the influence of their peer groups. We can distinguish here between:

- the friendship group, and
- peers in general; that is, other students around the same age.

The influence of a friendship group is likely to be far more intense. It may be augmented or, in some cases, reduced somewhat by the influence of 'peers in general.' Where the overall ethos of a school is positive, any negative influence of a friendship group may have a more limited effect.

It should certainly not be assumed that all or even most friendship groups influence their members to engage in bullying. Some groups are highly pro-social in their behaviour. The norms governing the behaviour of their members may be positive; they may influence individual members to treat those outside the group with respect. However, there are groups whose influence on their members is at times far from benign. Once the members of such groups get it into their heads that their group is in some way better or more important than those outside the group, there is a temptation to act so as to demonstrate their superiority. This can lead to bullying.

As suggested earlier, bullying can at times involve the whole group, as when members join together in a concerted attack on someone. In such cases there is an undifferentiated body of students; individual differences play little or no part. The mob is 'all together' – seemingly mindless, bent on satisfying some primitive impulse to participate in an orgy of aggression. Behind this behaviour one may discover strongly held prejudices, and a glorification of violence. Early social psychologists saw this behaviour as spreading through a kind of mindless 'contagion'.[6]

Such mobbing is motivated and sustained by aroused emotion rather than reason. As part of the group, the aggressors may feel anonymous and devoid of personal responsibility. We see this behaviour among 'soccer hooligans' intoxicated by their identification with a team or country. We see it when 'happy slapping' occurs and students take on the mob mentality which for a time they find exhilarating. Behind the scenes – in the planning of such acts – there *may* be ringleaders. Fortunately, this kind of scenario is relatively rare. In fact, the influence of a group, especially that of the friendship group, on bullying is generally less direct and less crude.

It can happen in a number of ways:

- **Members of a friendship group may come together in part because they share certain prejudices that appear to justify treating some of their peers badly.** With the support of the group, individuals are more able to give expression to their dislike for some other students by bullying them. They no longer need to suppress their antagonism. With the support of their mates they feel justified and can more effectively attack their enemies – and feel safer. The group may not act as a single entity, as in mobbing, but play a supportive role to individual members.

- **In cases where members did not initially feel negatively about some of their peers outside the group, they may in time come to do so.** They may be persuaded that students disliked by certain individuals in the group deserve to be treated badly. Once they have actually engaged in bullying someone who the group as a whole is thought to dislike, they may justify their actions to themselves. Rationalisations, if needed, come readily to mind. Once during a group discussion with teenagers I was given an explanation as to why a particular boy was bullied by the class. It's obvious, I was told, he's not like us: he isn't normal.
- **In taking part in actions approved by the group, members are reinforced for doing so and are likely to feel pleased about it.** They may come to identify more strongly with the group. Feelings of personal self-esteem become closely linked to the 'success' or otherwise of the group in becoming ever more dominant in the school environment. With each episode of successful bullying in which a group member has taken part, identification with the group grows and with it the self-esteem of the member. Bullying becomes a means of both self aggrandisement, and aggrandisement of the group.
- **Successfully participating in actions approved by the group may increase members' basic sense of security.** Their position or status in the group becomes more secure. They feel they belong. In some circumstances, members may fear that if they do not 'go along' with the group they will become targeted themselves. Hence members may at times seek to outdo each other in demonstrations of their commitment to acting as 'good' members should. This may be seen as the safest option.

In conceptualising the bully, practitioners of the Method of Shared Concern do not dismiss as irrelevant personal characteristics, or the personal beliefs or values that students may hold. What they do assert is that bullies do not conform to a single personality type, and may be motivated in different ways. Members of a group of students who engage in bullying someone may have notably different personal characteristics. One may perform the role of ringleader and present as a bold, confident, controlling, cold and manipulative type, admired or feared by other members of the group. Another member may strike one as good-natured, agreeable, affable, certainly *capable* of empathy for a person who is in distress, but enjoying group membership so much that on occasions – as when engaged in bullying someone – such feelings are suppressed. A third member may seem uneasy, anxious and generally unhappy about the situation, but motivated to go along with the bullying because it seems the safest thing to do. This member would be glad if the bullying stopped, but does not want other people – especially his or her friendship group – to know that. Figure 3 illustrates the heterogeneity of types one may sometimes encounter in groups that engage in bullying others. (We meet these characters again in chapter 3.)

Figure 3 A trio of suspected bullies

Going beyond these personality differences, the proponents of the method emphasise the power that group norms and group processes possess in determining and sustaining bullying behaviour. This is fundamental and applies to all the members, including the ringleader whose desire to dominate and bully is greatly amplified by the admiration received from the group.

The power of the group to which a person belongs continues to have an important influence throughout life, but is especially influential in childhood and adolescence. It can therefore be misleading to view the school bully as acting autonomously through the possession of a relatively stable personality that invariably determines his or her actions. The influence of the friendship group may be far more crucial.

The victim

By and large, people who become targeted by someone else are readily identifiable. Ask a class of students who tends to be bullied by others, and one can be sure that there will be a large consensus in identifying several students who tend to bear the brunt of a good deal of teasing or taunting. But there *are* cases that can be hard to fathom. Some students have been described as 'false victims'; that is, students who pretend to be victimised, either because they want to get attention or because they want to get somebody in trouble. Then there are students who are unusually sensitive to any kind of criticism, and those who react strongly to any kind of teasing, however mild. We should not, however, jump to the conclusion that such children do not need help of some kind. We may reasonably consider ways in which they can be helped to relate more constructively, or perhaps more robustly, to others. But clearly the kind of help they need is not the kind that is provided by the application of the Method of Shared Concern.

Just as we may have misleading stereotypes of the bully, so too we can have misleading stereotypes of the victim. Figure 4 shows a drawing in made by an anonymous Australian schoolboy which conveys his conception of what a victim is like.

Figure 4 A stereotypical victim

This depiction of the victim fits criteria suggested in the previous chapter. The victim is evidently less powerful than those who are verbally harassing him; he appears unable to defend himself adequately (being greatly outnumbered), and is clearly oppressed. Once again, however, the illustration captures only one kind of bullying, in this case direct verbal abuse. It also suggests, through caricature, that the victim is unusual in appearance and somewhat ridiculous. Finally, in the picture the target is the object of a concerted attack, rather than, as is often the case, being bullied by one or a few perpetrators.

Generalisations about the nature of the victim, like generalisations about the nature of the bully, can be misleading. Anyone can in some circumstances be a victim, just as anyone can in some circumstances act the part of the bully. However the *risk* of being bullied is generally greater if one is notably 'different' from most other people. Prejudiced thinking may lead to those who are 'different' being targeted.

Some differences are due to people belonging to fairly well defined groups, such as occurs when there are students of different ethnicity present at a school. Others are due to divergences in personality and behaviour. We can thus differentiate two kinds of difference, one due to divergent social characteristics, such as ethnicity, and the other due to divergent personal characteristics. These may be considered separately.

Differences due to group membership

Some groups are clearly defined; for example, those composed of students whose appearance or speech signify membership of a particular ethnic group. Commonly, if they are in a minority, these students can become the victims of ethnic or racial prejudice.[7] With respect to personality and behaviour they may be no different from other students, or the differences may be minimal. It is the fact that they belong to an identifiable social group against which there is significant prejudice that is crucial.

The victims may feel deeply offended and angry and, in some cases, depressed by the negative treatment they receive. However, if there is a relatively large number of students in the school who are like themselves and there is among these students a sense of togetherness, those victimised will have an important source of support, and, under such circumstances, their self-esteem and resilience may hardly be affected. Further, in some countries acts of racial discrimination incur legal sanctions, providing further support for such victims. This can also lessen the distress they feel. They may recognise that the negative treatment they receive from others is not due to any personal failing for which they might be personally ashamed.

This is not to dismiss the importance of bullying based on prejudice, but to recognise that it is in some respects different from that experienced by many other students who are victimised for personal reasons and cannot call upon much social support. Abuse clearly hurts less if it is not personal, and its effect is capable of being lessened when it is shared with a group who are receiving similar treatment.

Not all categories of persons are so defined that members can access and derive support from those who are in the same boat. For example, students who are bullied because they are thought to be gay constitute an ill-defined group.[8] A few of them may have a homosexual orientation that they openly acknowledge; others may prefer not to disclose, or may actually be quite unsure of, their sexuality; others may actually be heterosexual. Many of those who are the object of homophobic prejudice do not know to whom they may turn to get emotional support. Their plight is therefore often worse than that of the targets of ethnic prejudice. We should also bear in mind that being called 'gay' has for students a broader meaning, suggesting in boys a softness or gentleness of disposition, the antithesis of what is considered 'macho'. The boy who is called 'gay' may want to deny that he is what they say he is, or feel that it is somehow his *fault* for being like that – and despise himself. A girl who does not fit the ladylike gender stereotype may experience similar feelings. These students may be unmotivated to seek support from other people being victimised for the same reason.

In some schools gender differences may be the basis of bullying. Here we have a generally unambiguous category of difference, students being either male or female with (in most cases) approximately equal numbers in each category, at least in coeducational schools where harassment based on gender differences may occur. Many students of the same gender can be expected to offer support to a victim of gender-based harassment, and there is sometimes the possibility of invoking legal sanctions that may be applied to those who engage in such harassment. Nevertheless, we find that gender-based bullying is not uncommon in schools and can be distressing. Overwhelmingly it takes the form of boys harassing girls rather than vice-versa.[9]

As with other forms of bullying based on group membership, such as the targeting of students because of their social class or religious affiliation, the prevalence and severity of the bullying may depend on both community values and the role performed by teachers.

Differences due to individual characteristics

Almost any individual characteristic can be associated with being targeted at school, depending on the prejudices that exist in the school population. In one school a student may be bullied for being clever and achieving academic distinction; in another, such a student may be widely admired. Being chronically disabled may excite ridicule in one school, while in another, students may be largely sympathetic and supportive of such students. However, it remains true that the possession of identifiable personal characteristics that set students apart from others generally increases their risk of being bullied.

Some characteristics that may put a child at risk are physical; for example, being unusually short or unusually tall, or having poor eyesight or defective hearing. Children with deformities of face or body are sometimes cruelly teased. Some psychological characteristics suggesting abnormality attract bullying. These include evidence of mental slowness, Asperger syndrome, attention deficit hyperactivity disorder (ADHD) and Tourette syndrome. Children whose behaviour is within what is called the 'normal' range may nevertheless have characteristics that lead to them being bullied. These include submissiveness or awkwardness in social interactions, social introversion, extreme shyness, loudness and insensitivity to others and, especially, an inability to make friends.[10]

Personal vulnerability

As with the tendency to bully, research has established that there are various correlates of being victimised at school, including those discussed above. Again, however, the correlations, though significant, are not high. It would appear that the possession of certain characteristics does not *guarantee* that a person will be bullied at school. Far from it. We may at times wonder why it is that children we expect to be vulnerable are not bullied, and those whom we expect not to be bullied sometimes are.

One answer to this question is that the possession of one quality that puts a person at risk may be compensated for by another characteristic that reduces his or her vulnerability. Shortness of stature, for example, is one correlate of being bullied[11]; but there have been many short men who were highly dominant, for instance Napoleon. There are children who are quite introverted and withdrawn whom others hesitate to bully because they are big, strong and known to respond aggressively if tormented. Some children who are physically weak and puny inspire such affection and support from others that no-one wishes to harm them. To get a reliable picture of who is most vulnerable we need a knowledge of a range of characteristics and how they are viewed by other students.

Is vulnerability 'fixed'?

The short answer is that some kinds of vulnerability are more or less fixed; for instance, some cases of severe intellectual disability and some incurable physical weaknesses or limitations (although it is important to recognise that some students who appear to be highly vulnerable may learn to act or react in ways that reduce their vulnerability).[12] With many students, reducing vulnerability to bullying *can* be achieved, especially if they are helped to do so by others. But unless some efforts are made to reduce a student's vulnerability, by the student or others, there is a strong probability that he or she will be vulnerable for life. Reports from experimental geneticists and educational psychologists sometimes paint a pessimistic picture. There is, for example, evidence of a significant genetic influence predisposing a child to be bullied.[13] There is also evidence that children who are bullied at school are more likely than others to be bullied in the workplace.[14] These findings should prepare us to recognise that if students who are vulnerable are not helped, or do not help themselves – for instance through assertiveness training or improving their capacity to make friends – the outlook for them is far from bright, at least in social environments in which bullying is prevalent; and this appears to include all schools, some workplaces and some homes.

'Innocent' and 'provocative' victims

It is certainly common to characterise victims as particularly helpless individuals who are repeatedly exposed to situations with which they cannot cope. We are apt to call them 'passive' victims or 'innocent' victims. But are all victims really 'innocent'?

It is in fact sensible to differentiate between two categories of victim. Taking for the moment an outsider perspective, we may recognise a targeted child as an 'innocent' victim. In our judgement, that is, the victim in no way deserves to be bullied. He or she has done nothing at all to provoke or justify the victimisation. By contrast, there are so-called 'provocative' victims who go out of their way to annoy others and then complain if they are themselves treated badly. Recently I encountered a case of bullying in Australia undertaken by some Italian students who had been the butt of racial insults and abuse from an Australian boy, whom they began to bully. The provocation was real; the response was (I thought) unduly severe, quite disproportionately so, persistent – and needing to be stopped. However, the circumstances in this case were different from those in many others in which there had been no apparent provocation.

It should not be assumed that a high proportion of students who have been identified as victims are provocative. Estimates are difficult to make because what may seem provocative to one person can be construed as legitimate assertiveness to another. One estimate is that they constitute 10 per cent of all students who have been categorised as victims.[15] Yet experience in working with students using the Method of Shared Concern indicates that it is not an insignificant number – especially if we include students whose 'provocation' is not intentional.

These two types, the innocent victim and the provocative victim, often need to be treated somewhat differently in the course of applying the Method of

Shared Concern. Broadly, we may identify the innocent victim as one for whom there is no evidence at all that he or she has done anything that would justify counter-aggressive behaviour. Such a person is often (though not always) rather introverted, meek, anxious and unhappy. The provocative victim is *likely* to be more extraverted, aggressive, hostile, insensitive to others, disturbed and with few, if any, friends.

We should bear in mind, however, that some students are *seen* as being provocative when this is not the case. Bullies may see a slight where none was intended. There may be something about the way the victim behaves that appears provocative. The victim's very appearance, her grating voice, his annoying accent, the way she walks, his sheer impudence in thinking he is as good as we are; all these and more may show that the target was 'asking for it' – and the bully duly obliges. The perpetrators are in the wrong. But we must nevertheless understand just how *they* see things.

What has been said about the behaviour of bullies being greatly influenced by peer groups is also true of victims of bullying. In their case their behaviour can be a result of being continually undermined by the wider peer group, with whom they appear not to 'fit in'. They also tend to lack acceptance and support from a more intimate group. Even those they call friends may be ambivalent. They may come to regard the negative judgements made about them as unshakably valid. They may begin to agree with those who label them as losers. As research has shown, having a low level of self-esteem appears to elicit bullying from others.[16]

Implications of how bullies and victims are conceptualised

In examining what is known about students who are frequently involved in bully/victim problems it is evident that one can easily be misled by stereotypes, whether the stereotype be of the bully or the victim. It is therefore important to separate the stereotypes from what has been found to be the case empirically.

The 'bully' is often seen as essentially vile and unredeemable, deserving to be punished and only controllable through the use of punishment. Here, for example, are some of the adjectives applied to the bully by a prominent expert on bullying: 'vile', 'vicious', 'devious', 'glib', 'shallow', 'superficial', 'slippery', 'slimy', 'ingratiating', 'fawning', 'toadying', 'obsequious', 'sycophantic', 'untrustworthy', 'evasive', 'narcissistic', 'petty', 'greedy', 'fraudulent', 'arrogant', 'mean-spirited', 'selfish', 'insensitive', 'cunning', 'scheming', 'deluded' and 'demonic'.[17]

Arguably some of these epithets may be applied to some individual bullies (and also to some non-bullies). They can hardly be said to apply to all students who bully. It is difficult to see how anyone could work constructively with someone who had all these qualities. Yet it is not unusual for bullies to be seen in this way, especially by people who have learned to fear them.

Some explanations have been offered as to why bullies are seen in this way. The answer Pikas gives is that there is in all of us a tendency to demonise those who threaten us and whom we identify as 'the enemy'. To a lesser or greater extent there appears to be in all of us a predisposition to regard those who bully as evil; sometimes they are likened to rapists and murderers. Some attribute the tendency to demonise bullies to the existence in humans, as in all mammals, of an ancient reptilian brain which sits atop the spinal column (see figure 5): a remnant from our prehistoric, evolutionary past.[18]

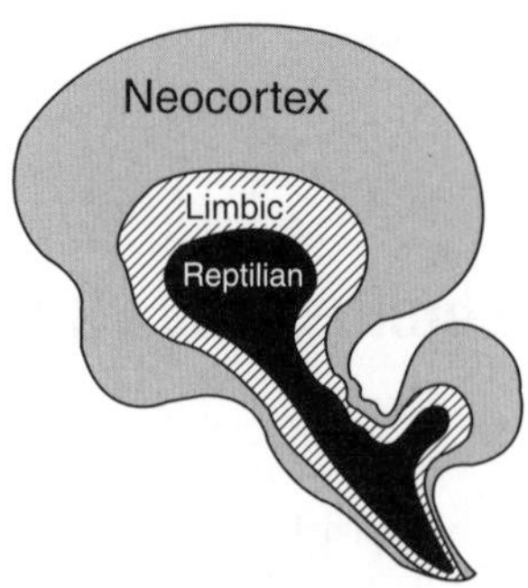

Figure 5 Simplified brain structure

This is seen as responsible for our drive to establish and defend territory, fuelled by an extremely potent 'will to power'. The more recently developed neo-cortex provides us with the means – but unfortunately at times not the energy or will – to rein in the rampant primitive urges.

Other researchers have implicated the limbic system in the brain, more especially the amygdala, as the source of the emotions that drive us to act aggressively. The very thought of a bully – especially one who might bully us – throws us into a rage.

Others, following the Swiss psychiatrist Jung[19], have eschewed physiological explanations and have attributed the tendency to demonise those who threaten us to the existence of an archetype; that is, a psychological structure of which we are normally unconscious that developed during our evolutionary past and under some circumstance may act as an imperative, seeking fulfilment in action. Confronted with a 'bully' the archetype of the enemy is activated and we see red.

Whatever the explanation, it follows that it must be exceedingly difficult to work with and change the behaviour of someone we have so emphatically demonised. Fortunately, as we have seen, there is evidence that the stereotype is a distortion of reality. It may be conceded that some, a small minority, of students who bully are psychopathic and need intensive psychotherapy. Some others certainly may be hard to work with. But, as exponents of the Method of Shared Concern believe, a very large proportion of those who bully are not saddled with a personality that makes it virtually impossible for them to respond positively, for instance, to an invitation to act constructively, especially when they come to see that it is in their interest to do so. Further, it is evident that the personality of the individual student is often less of a determining factor in bringing about bullying than the influence of the group to which the 'bully' belongs. Focusing exclusively on the demonised bully prevents an acknowledgement of this fact.

Stereotyping the victim can also be counterproductive. Here the tendency is to portray the victim as both innocent and impotent. That the victim is not invariably innocent has become clear with the recognition that some victims are indeed provocative. Similarly, it is evident that skills of self-assertion can be taught and utilised by some victims in some situations.

There are two dangers here. One is to blame the victim for not being assertive; the other is to deny the possibility that the victim can learn to be more assertive and more effective interpersonally. Exponents of the Method of Shared Concern recognise that there are indeed provocative victims whose behaviour needs to change, and that it is not unrealistic to expect students who are being bullied to explore what they can do to solve the problem – and, where possible, acquire the necessary interpersonal skills. Again, as in the case of the bully, it is recognised that how students behave, and how their behaviour can be changed, is embedded in group processes; and these need to be understood before positive changes can be brought about.

Endnotes

1. Greater physical prowess is demonstrably a factor in facilitating bullying behaviour, especially among boys (Olweus, 1993).
2. Relatively high average scores on psychoticism (a measure of emotional insensitivity) on the Eysenck Personality Inventory have been reported for students identified as 'bullies' (Slee & Rigby, 1993). Students who bully have also been found to score higher than others on a measure of machiavellianism (Sutton & Keogh, 2001). Other studies of the personality characteristics of bullies are summarised in Rigby (2002).
3. Negative relations with parents have been reported as characteristic of many students who continually engage in bullying (see Rigby, 1993, 2008).
4. Solberg and Olweus (2003) have provided this estimate based upon large samples of Norwegian students.
5. In an international survey of 11 to 15-year-olds from 15 different countries it was reported that bully–victims experienced worse emotional adjustment than any other subgroup of students (Nansel et al 2001).
6. The notion that in the context of the crowd individuals may lose their capacity to act responsibly and act as a mob was first advanced by the French social psychologist Le Bon in 1895.
7. Some minority ethnic groups are subjected to a disproportionate amount of bullying in schools; for example, Australian Aboriginal students in Australia (Rigby, 2002).
8. The most comprehensive study to date in the United States revealed that young people between the ages of 14 and 22 who identified as gay or lesbian were significantly more likely than others to be bullied by peers (Berlan et al., 2010).
9. In a large study of approximately 14,000 Australian coeducational school students who reported having been bullied at school, girls were 10 times more likely than boys to indicate that they had been bullied by a member of the opposite sex (Rigby, 1998a).
10. Reported correlates of being bullied at school are summarised in Rigby (2002).
11. A survey conducted in England indicated that short students are more at risk of being bullied at school than others (Voss & Mulligan, 2000).
12. While young people who are seen as mentally retarded are more likely than others to be bullied, some evidently are not. According to Nettelbeck and Wilson (2002), those who have learned not to react strongly to verbal teasing are much less likely to be victimised.

13. A comprehensive study of over a thousand families with twins aged 10 years has shown that children's genetic endowments, as well as their environments, influence which children become victims, bullies and bully–victims (Ball et al., 2008).
14. Adults who were bullied in the workplace have reported that they were bullied by peers more frequently than others at school (Smith, 1997).
15. See Solberg and Olweus (2003).
16. Egan and Perry (1998) have demonstrated in a longitudinal study that among American primary school students low self-esteem was a 'cause' of being bullied as well as a consequence.
17. These are terms employed by the anti-bullying activist Tim Field in describing the character of the workplace bully (see <http://www.bullyonline.org/workbully/serial.htm>).
18. For example, Koestler (1967) popularised the idea that the aggressive behaviour of humans was largely determined by the nature of the brain, especially by its inherited reptilian base, and argued that this posed a major obstacle to preventing war between nations.
19. Carl Jung (1875–1961) argued that we tend to project the dark side or shadow in our own nature onto those we fear and treat them as enemies whom we wish to destroy. See Jung (1981).

Part 2 How the Method of Shared Concern works

The Method of Shared Concern operates by working with, rather than against, those who are involved in cases of bullying. It takes a positive view of human nature, even of the nature of those who are customarily labelled as bullies. It assumes that if perpetrators and their targets are approached and worked with in the 'right' way, conflict between them can usually be resolved peacefully. The right way emphatically does not involve the use or the threat of punishment.

How the method works can be described in terms of the procedural steps to be taken by practitioners. These are detailed in this section. But beyond that, it requires an understanding or insight into the human condition and the group dynamics that make its success possible. This understanding may grow with practice. But can its development be assisted through study and reflection? Pikas has embarked on the writing of a novel that seeks to promote a deeper understanding of the essence of his approach.[1]

The Method of Shared Concern is *not* ideologically driven. It accepts that some cases of bullying are not appropriately dealt with using this method. Such cases include those that manifest violence or involve criminal behaviour. It accepts that there may be other cases in which the method will not work; but these are few. Importantly, it takes a solid stand that those who bully will not be permitted to continue to do so. As a last resort, the school may have to take disciplinary action and the bully prevented from having contact with the victim. The victim is to be protected at all cost.

Despite these concessions, the claim made by the exponents of the Method of Shared Concern is that the process presently to be described is:

- the most **consistent** with what is now known about the social psychology of school bullying
- the most **developed and comprehensive** of all existing approaches to the problem
- the most **effective** in getting the bullying stopped
- above all, the most **likely to ensure the safety** of the victim.

These large and – some may say – extravagant claims will be carefully examined in chapter 5.

Our concern in this section is with what the practitioner of the Method of Shared Concern does in working first with individual students and then, when progress has been made, with groups of students.

Clearly the first step is to select cases of bullying that can be handled appropriately using this method. In chapter 3 we consider the criteria that may lead to the identification of such cases; then we examine in detail how a practitioner of the method conducts a series of interviews with *individual students* who are thought to have been involved in some way with the bullying, as suspected bullies or as victims.

In chapter 4, we turn our attention to how practitioners of the method who have already worked with students individually subsequently engage with students *in groups* to discuss ways in which the problem can be finally resolved. This chapter concludes with a summary of the process of applying the Method of Shared Concern.

Endnote

1. Pikas wrote in a letter to me: 'I have failed to achieve publication of articles where I explain the components of the shared concern paradigm that work both at micro and macro levels of mediation. My friends have explained: you are concentrating too much stuff into a too small space. So I have divided a complex structure into discoveries made by four individuals – two women and two males in different ages – in a novel. They meet and found The *New Pickwick club* where they, discussing their experiences, bring forward the elements of shared concern that lead to shared solutions. I have reproduced at my home-site (1) a summary of their adventures and (2) chapter 20, where the New Pickwick club members are gathered [for the] first time. One of the members, a female medical student, 22, who has been a deputy teacher, tells others about her class discussion with teenagers that led to the Shared Concern method, that she practised next day. If you take a look at http://www.pikas.se/scm/ you may find some of the deep insights into SCm that the New Pickwick club members [had] at that meeting!'

Chapter 3 Meetings with individual students

Before the method is applied certain conditions should be fulfilled:

- There is **acceptance by the school** that the method *may* be used.
- The would-be practitioner is **adequately informed and trained** in the use of the method.
- An **appropriate case** has come to light.

Acceptance of the method should only be reached after it has been fully explained to the staff, and agreement has been reached about its use in *some selected* cases of bullying at the school. A school-based workshop should centre on its use, employing role playing of interactions between trainee practitioners and suspected bullies and victims. This should be run by an educator who is fully conversant with the method. There is now a useful DVD that provides additional help.[1] If there are significant reservations about the employment of the method in a school then it should not be employed.

Cases for which the method is to be used should be selected carefully. As stated earlier, cases of assault and criminal behaviour are unsuitable. Likewise, relatively mild cases may be more appropriately – and more speedily – resolved through informal counselling.

Bear in mind that the degree of severity of a case of bullying is sometimes not at first evident. A case seemingly suitable for one form of intervention may, with a better understanding of the situation, be dealt with in a different way. What appeared relatively mild may, as more is learned about a case, be recognised as being much more severe. Practitioners may reasonably change their minds about what method they choose to employ or continue with.

The targeted student

We must never forget that the safety and wellbeing of the targeted student is the primary aim of interventions in cases of school bullying. The Method of Shared Concern can be applied when two things come to light:

- a student is **seriously distressed**, *and*
- there are grounds for believing that an **identifiable group of students** have deliberately sought to cause the distress.

The combination of these factors is essential. This is not to say that distressed students should not be of concern to a school whatever the cause of their distress, only that the cause may not be bullying. The detection of distress in a student is the starting point.

A variety of signs may suggest bullying (see table 2). Some of these are more likely to be observed by a parent; some by a teacher or peer.

Table 2 Signs that a student is being bullied

Physical	Unexplained bruises, scratches or cuts Torn or damaged clothes or belongings
Psychosomatic	Non-specific pains, headaches, abdominal pains, mouth sores
School-related behaviours	Fear of walking to or from school. Change of route to school Fear of travelling on the school bus Asking to be driven to school Unwillingness to go to school Deterioration in school work Coming home hungry (because lunch money was taken) Reporting loss of possessions Asking for or stealing money (to pay the bully)
Changes in social behaviour	Having fewer friends Not wanting to go out Being invited out much less often
Emotional indicators	Appearing upset, unhappy, lonely, tearful, distressed Becoming withdrawn and depressed Unexpected mood swings Suicidal thinking Threatening or attempting suicide.
Worrying behaviours	Irritability and temper outbursts Not eating, overeating, being unable to sleep, nightmares, bed-wetting, crying out during sleep.
Indicators of poor health	Being generally tired or 'run-down' Low resistance to infection and recurring illnesses.

The most evident indications are likely to be signs of depression and profound discouragement and a retreat into a self-absorbed world of misery, as illustrated in figure 6.

Figure 6 The targeted student

It is true that one can never be sure that the distressful state of a student is due to bullying. Depression can strike seemingly without a cause. However, close observations of how the student is being treated can generally determine whether the depression is likely to have been induced or exacerbated through bullying. Bear in mind that bullying can take a wide variety of forms (see table 1 on page 4), and sometimes the least observable are the most distressing. Drawing upon observations reported by sympathetic bystanders, teachers, parents and the distressed student can normally confirm whether the distress is related to being bullied.

Identifying the participants

The practitioner must start by identifying, as far as possible, the students who have been involved in the bully/victim problem. We have reviewed above the signs that may lead to a suspicion that a student is being bullied. Compelling evidence is needed before the practitioner can begin, and this must be obtained from as many reliable sources as possible. Identifying all those who may have contributed to the bullying is often more difficult. Here it should be recognised that we are not seeking 'proof', only probable involvement. No accusations are made, no convictions are sought. The primary aim is to engage with students who are *suspected* of having taken part and to gain their cooperation. After listening to reports – and in some cases having observed the bullying – the practitioner can usually be confident that some if not all of the students selected for the application of the method have played a significant part in the bullying.

Why begin with meeting students individually?

Theoretically there is a choice. The students can be interviewed as a group or they can be interviewed one by one. The Method of Shared Concern, however, requires that initial interviews be conducted with individuals; more precisely, first with each of the suspected bullies, then with the person they have targeted. Why should this be?

The reason for interviewing the suspected bullies individually is psychological. It is possible to establish a much closer and more influential relationship with a person in a one-to-one meeting than with that person as part of a group. This is especially so when the group consists of students who have been bullying someone. Typically they feel that they have the strength in numbers to be able to defy the authority figure, and that it is in their interest to maintain unity. Older secondary students are more likely to act defiantly and make things difficult for the teacher. The task of establishing and maintaining a trusting relationship with an individual student is generally much easier for the teacher in a one-to-one situation.

The practice of meeting with the suspected bullies in a group is nevertheless employed in some intervention strategies. Certainly, if a teacher can achieve a breakthrough with individuals assembled as a group there is the obvious advantage of economising on time, which is often at a premium in schools. It would appear that *some* teachers with *some* students are able to do this effectively.[2] Unfortunately this is not the case for a great number of teachers, or in relation to many students who engage in bullying. For many teachers, confronting a group of students – especially adolescent students who are engaging in bullying – to gain their active cooperation is not only stressful but extremely difficult to undertake successfully. Most teachers recognise that progress can be made more readily when those who have bullied someone are spoken with individually.

Why not see the target first?

At first sight it seems reasonable for the practitioner to see the target first, as is the case when the Support Group Method is employed.[3] If you engage with the targeted student first you are able to obtain a first-hand account of what has been happening and how the target has been affected. Information is also normally forthcoming about who the bullies are. However, the exponents of the Method of Shared Concern take a different view. They do so largely because they believe that it is much safer for the target if he or she has *not talked first* with the practitioner and probably disclosed the names of the bullies. There are then no grounds for recrimination.

Two other reasons are sometimes given. The first is that factual information about the bullying (which might be picked up from the target) is not of central importance to the practitioner. The practitioner is more concerned with the perceptions of those who have taken part in the bullying than in objective facts that could be used to make a case against the bullies. The method does not aim at securing a 'conviction'. The second reason is that when the target is eventually seen it becomes possible to disclose that there is some good news; that some, if not all of the suspected bullies have agreed to help in bringing the bullying to an end. This is important in gaining the goodwill and cooperation of the target who might otherwise have been reluctant to receive help.

It must be acknowledged that ensuring that the suspected bullies are seen first is not always possible. The target may have actually come to see the practitioner and have described what has happened.[4] The target's parents may have contacted the school and perhaps also the practitioner. The practitioner may have actually seen the bullying taking place. Numerous sources of information may have been received confirming the occurrence of bullying.

The 'suspected bully'

Throughout the description of the application of the method, reference will be made to the 'suspected bully.' It is important to see why this is done.

If we take the view that a student is a proven bully, two things may follow. First, the student is conceived of as guilty, and in the eyes of many deserves to be punished. Gaining his or her unforced cooperation in 'fixing' the problem becomes difficult, if not impossible. Second, if *accusations* are made to the effect that the student has acted improperly or committed a misdemeanour, parental involvement becomes necessary. Proponents of the Method of Shared Concern believe that a solution to the problem can be achieved without parental involvement, especially if the school adopts an approach designed to empower the suspected bullies to solve the problem themselves. This does not mean that parents should be kept in the dark. As we shall see, the school needs to take steps to help parents understand how it is dealing with bully/victim problems.

When the evidence that the suspected bully has indeed engaged in bullying the target appears overwhelming, the practitioner needs to be especially careful. A natural temptation is to insist that the suspected bully 'admits it'. This would invalidate the approach. The suspected bully becomes defensive or distant, and the chances of unforced cooperation are greatly diminished. Under these circumstances the practitioner must act as if the student is no different from those about whom there is no compelling evidence. It is well to bear in mind that one's primary concern is with understanding the perceptions of the suspected bully as a step towards bringing about an agreed solution to the problem.

Finally, all this does not mean that it must not emerge in the meetings that bullying has taken place. The practitioner and the suspected bully may actually acknowledge that bullying has occurred. This happens quite often – but the emergence of this understanding is not to be forced.

Meetings with individual students in context

Let us consider now what the practitioner is seeking to achieve through interviews with the individuals who are thought to have played a role in the bullying: the suspected bullies and the target.

Essentially the interviews are intended to prepare the students for subsequent group meetings in which the resolution of the problem will be planned and finally put into effect. There is a temptation to solve the problem as quickly as possible simply through the meetings *just with individual students*. This is a mistake. We may well think that this first stage is sufficient. Yet despite early assurances from those interviewed, the bullying may still continue. The individual interviews should be viewed as steps towards an end, not an end in themselves.

Remember that the group meetings become feasible only after the suspected bullies have acknowledged the plight of the person about whom the practitioner has shared a concern, have undertaken to act in a helpful way and have actually demonstrated that they have done so. Once it is clearly understood what part the individual meetings play in advancing the method, preparations can be made to begin the first phase.

The first meeting with a suspected bully

Having identified a number of students who are likely to have taken part in the bullying, or to have supported it in some way, each one is seen in turn, starting with the likely ringleader (if known). Under some circumstances, if desired, other students acutely aware of the problem, such as bystanders, may be included, as they may sometimes play an important role in influencing the bullying. The number of students seen varies, but is commonly around three or four. There is generally no need to extend numbers much beyond this.

The interview should take place in private and where there will be no interruptions. It can be expected to last for at least ten minutes, sometimes longer.

The practitioner has a number of specific goals in mind for this first meeting with a suspected bully:

1. that the suspected bully **understands the role being taken by the practitioner**: that is, to help students in general to feel safe at the school, and to help one student in particular about whom the practitioner is presently concerned

2. that the suspected bully **acknowledges that that student is really having a hard time at school**
3. that the suspected bully is **ready to help in some way** to improve the situation, and states what action he or she is prepared to take to help
4. that the suspected bully **understands that he or she will in the near future be interviewed again** to monitor progress, and that a number of **other students are also being asked to help**
5. that the practitioner **gains some understanding of how the suspected bully views the situation, and his or her relationships with other students**. (With successive interviews, knowledge of the group situation and its dynamic is expected to deepen, and this will assist the practitioner in bringing about a successful resolution of the problem.)

These goals are to be realised without coercion or compulsion on the part of the practitioner.

The practitioner's state of mind

The success of this method depends primarily on the attitude of the practitioner toward each of the suspected bullies. If the practitioner feels angry and vengeful, often a perfectly understandable state of mind, the method cannot work; likewise, if the interviewer is fearful and is apt to be dominated by the suspected bully. Feeling intimidated by the suspected bullies does sometimes occur, and such fearfulness needs to be overcome. The practitioner must not be emotionally detached and robot-like either, or nothing useful will be disclosed. The practitioner must convey a genuine concern not only for the victim but also for the suspected bully. It should be understood that the suspected bully may feel constrained in what he or she can say by a sense of loyalty to the friendship group or by a fear of what they might say or do if too much is revealed. Further, the suspected bully may not be entirely trusting of the practitioner. Throughout, the practitioner must keep clearly in mind what he or she is trying to achieve in using the method, while being continually open and sensitive to what the suspected bullying is saying and feeling.

In order to improve the situation for everyone concerned, it is essential that the practitioner understands where the bully is coming from. This requires a suspension of *immediate judgement*. This can be difficult.

Teachers and instructors are programmed to a large extent to tell others what they should know and what they must do. This must be avoided or suppressed when a teacher or counsellor adopts the role of a practitioner of the Method of Shared Concern. It is tempting to include at the meeting instruction on, or at least clarification of, what is meant by 'bullying,' how it can be identified and the harm it does.[5] This can and should be appropriately conveyed and discussed in classrooms with *all* students as part of the school curriculum. But it is out of place when the method is actually being applied.

In fact, the normal pedagogic orientation – to teach and (sometimes) to preach – can be counterproductive. It places the student in the role of mostly passive listener. He or she is being asked to listen to much of the 'usual thing' from a teacher. True, knowledge of what constitutes bullying is important, but the immediate need is to make a genuine contact with the person before you. You are seeking to bring about a constructive relationship with the bully – for the sake of the bully as well as for the sake of the victim. The nineteenth-century existentialist writer Soren Kierkegaard said what was needed if we want to help anyone:

> *If real success is to attend the effort to bring a man [or a child] to a definite position, one must first of all take pains to find him where he is and begin there.*[6]

This is rarely done. The starting point with the bully is often: 'Look, see what you have done wrong! What are you going to do about it?'

Kierkegaard goes on:

> *In order to help another effectively I must understand more than he – yet first of all surely I must understand what he understands. If I do not know that, my greater understanding will be of no help to him. If, however, I am disposed to plume myself on my greater understanding it is because I am vain or proud, so that at bottom, instead of benefitting him, I want to be admired. But all true effort to help begins with self-humiliation: the helper must first humble himself under him he would*

help, and therewith must understand that to help does not mean to be sovereign but to be a servant, that to help does not mean to be ambitious but to be patient, that to help means to endure for the time being the imputation that one is in the wrong and does not understand what the other understands.

Finally Kierkegaard turns to the case of someone who is angry and is really in the wrong – the 'typical' bully.

Take the case of a man [or child] who is passionately angry, and let us assume that he really is in the wrong. Unless you can begin with him by making it seem as if it were he that had to instruct you, and unless you can do it in such a way that the angry man, who was too impatient to listen to a word of yours, is glad to discover in you a complaisant and attentive listener – if you cannot do that, you cannot help him at all.

Emphatically, the aim of the teacher is *not* to find reasons for excusing the bully. But unless the art of listening is practised in the course of interacting with a bully the teacher will not be dealing with the actual person who is there, but rather with an abstraction bearing little relation to reality.

This humility – and apparent self-abasement, even – is a necessary part of the mindset of the practitioner as he or she listens to how each suspected bully sees the situation. Pikas has often suggested that the role model who best exemplifies the ideal practitioner is the television detective Lieutenant Columbo, as portrayed by Peter Falk.[7] Columbo is anything but imposing. He is deeply respectful and seemingly not over-bright; but he is a careful listener and he doesn't miss a clue.

This is not to suggest that the practitioner must agree with whatever the suspected bully is saying. In describing the Method of Shared Concern to others, I have sometimes heard it suggested that the practitioner is really a supporter of the bullies and implicitly supports the bullying. Nothing could be further from the truth. Whatever 'support' is given to suspected bullies is to enable them to express honestly what they feel and think, and to enable the practitioner to work with them towards a realistic solution.

The interview

The practitioner greets the suspected bully in a warm but non-effusive manner and invites him or her to sit in a chair opposite (without an intervening desk), then waits for eye contact before the interaction begins.

The practitioner first explains his or her role – to help children feel safe at school – then points out that it has been noticed that a particular student has been having a hard time at school with other students. The practitioner may briefly describe what has been discovered about the plight of this student; for example, being upset, being isolated or staying away from school. No reference is made to any bullying. The practitioner's concern for the target must be sincerely conveyed before the suspected bully is asked what he or she has noticed or knows about the target's situation (see figure 7).

Figure 7 Practitioner and suspected bully: 'It looks like Tom is having a hard time at school.'

Note that the practitioner is not trying to 'get to the bottom of the matter' or to apportion blame, but rather to elicit a constructive response that will help to change the situation. Bullying may or may not be mentioned by the suspected bully. It is *not* brought up by the practitioner.

As soon as the student has acknowledged some awareness (not guilt) relating to how the target is feeling, he or she is asked directly *what can be done to help improve matters.*

Commonly, the student makes helpful suggestions about what can be done. But if he or she does not, the practitioner may make suggestions, ones that are not difficult to carry out. Strong approval is expressed for any constructive proposals that the student makes, or agrees to. It is important that whatever action is agreed to is what the student genuinely wants to undertake.

In the course of discussing the matter with the suspected bully, the practitioner should be seeking to discover how the student sees the situation, without probing for the objective facts. Conversation commonly turns to how the suspected bully sees others in his or her friendship group, and their possible involvement in what has been happening. Always bear in mind that the suspected bully may be strongly influenced by other members of the group. Understanding his or her relationships with group members could be important in helping to solve the problem. The practitioner should not, however, pump the suspected bully for such information. It should come out naturally as a consequence of the practitioner showing a genuine interest.

Sometimes the practitioner may suspect that the student is being constrained by the group or a member of the group to support the bullying, and has misgivings about what he or she is actually doing; or the suspected bully may be afraid of going against the group or the ringleader by not 'going along'. It is not up to the practitioner to interrogate the suspected bully to seek confirmation that either of these is the case. If it comes out, well and good. It must not be forced. Whatever the practitioner discerns about the suspected bully's state of mind and his or her relations with other members of the group can be helpful in working towards an eventual solution.

How the meeting concludes is important. The suspected bully should be aware that other members of the friendship group will be (or have been) spoken with and asked to help, and that there is no intention to punish anyone. The student should be thanked for what he or she has promised to do. At the same time, it is made clear that a further meeting will be held with the student to discover what progress has been made. A time and place for such a meeting is arranged.

There is normally no need for the meeting to be prolonged. Most of the time should be taken in the practitioner *listening* to the suspected bully.

Here is an example – with a commentary – of a possible interaction between a practitioner and a suspected bully. The suspected bully is about 13 years old and in the same class as the person who appears to have been targeted by him and his friends.

Example: Interview with a suspected bully

Phase one

Practitioner (P): Good morning. Thank you for coming along to see me. Please sit down. [*After establishing eye-contact*]: My role in the school is to help keep students safe, to make sure they are not upset by things that are happening to them [*this is said in a matter-of-fact way, in no way accusingly*].

I hear that one student, Tom, has been having a hard time at school recently. He's been looking upset, crying and unable to concentrate on his lessons. And he's been staying away from school. He's been in a bad way. I am getting concerned about him. [*After a pause*]: I am going to be talking to a number of students about him.

It is possible that at this stage the student may feel under scrutiny, and may ask whether he or she is in trouble. If so, P makes it clear that that is not the case. Nobody is in trouble. Some students will need more reassurance than others.

I gather that you know Tom. [*Waits for acknowledgement.*] I'd like you to help me understand what has been happening to him. What have you noticed yourself about him lately? [*Long pause. P waits.*]

Suspected bully (SB): Well, he does sometimes seem a bit down. Some kids have been teasing him. Just having fun. Nothing much.

This may not be an altogether accurate disclosure. But P does not dig for more information. This is sufficient for the next step.

P: So it does seem that things aren't so good for him right now.

SB: I suppose so.

The first stage has been achieved. SB has acknowledged that the situation for Tom is not so good. There may be no sense of remorse, but there may well be the recognition of a social obligation to help.

Phase two

P: I am wondering if there is anything you can think of that could make things a bit better for Tom. [*Long pause. P waits.*]

SB: Well, I suppose I could stop making fun of him – like calling him names.

Here SBs may give a variety of responses, ranging from a non-committal 'I don't know what I could do', to a slightly more positive 'just leave him alone', to a much more positive 'try to be nice to him'. Very rarely does the SB assert that he or she is not prepared to do anything.

P [*enthusiastically – not grudgingly*]: That would be excellent. So you are going to stop teasing him. That's a good start.

Depending on how the relationship between P and SB is developing, the interview might proceed as follows:

P: What about other kids in your group? What are they like?

Here P attempts to get SB talking about the 'others'. P must show genuine interest in what SB says and thinks about them, in no way criticising any of them. This is where P needs to listen most carefully and pick up cues about how SB is feeling about other members of the group and the role he or she is playing. At some point it may be appropriate to suggest that SB have a word with one or other of them about Tom needing help, but only if there are grounds for thinking that this would be an acceptable thing to do. In any case it should never be insisted upon.

P: Well, thank you very much for talking with me. I appreciate your help and your undertaking to stop teasing Tom and having a word with X [*if this has been agreed*]. Now let's arrange to meet again to see how things are going. [*A time and place are agreed upon.*] Nice talking with you.

Some variations

- **SB may deny knowledge of what has gone on.** This may be due to genuine ignorance, but is more likely (if sound preliminary work has been done) to be due to an unreadiness to cooperate. P can briefly change the subject. If the target (T) is, or *has been*, part of the friendship group with SB, or takes part in any activities with SB, P may ask about what they do, (or did), together, then return to the subject of T's current condition, and how he or she seems to be these days. (This may enable the student to recognise any change that has occurred, and provide an opportunity to acknowledge some concern.)
- **SB may say that he or she has no idea what can be done.** To help, P may make some suggestions; ones that are easy to agree with, such as keeping an eye on what is happening to T and not adding to T's problems.
- **SB may deny any personal responsibility but mention one of the group who may have upset T.** When this happens, P may suggest that SB have a word with that person. P may say something like: 'Well, you have some influence with X. I wonder if you could have a word with her. I think she would listen to what you might say.'

- **SB may feel some justification in upsetting T**, especially if there has been a degree of provocation. In such cases P should listen uncritically – acknowledging that that is how SB sees it. This does not mean that P agrees with SB's judgement. Having listened attentively, P should reiterate the concern that has been shared with SB about T's plight, and again question what can be done about it. SB may argue that T must also start behaving differently. P can accept that this *may* be so – but continue to ask for and reinforce any positive suggestions.

  If it becomes clear that SB feels that T must also change in some ways before progress can be made, P may ask SB to make a suggestion that T might accept as a step towards a solution.
- **SB may pressure P to say why he or she has been chosen to be interviewed.** The answer must be that SB has been chosen because it is thought that he or she could help, not because of any accusations being made. P should never get into an argument over this. Return to the main theme; that is, T is having a hard time and needs 'our' help.

If no progress is made, it may be necessary to say: 'Well, it seems like you haven't noticed anything or you don't want to talk about it today. Please keep your eye out for anything – and we'll talk again later.'

A common mistake is to *assume* the student has engaged in the bullying behaviour and must be pressured to acknowledge a real concern for the target. Using this method, it is quite wrong to ask suspected bullies how they would feel if they had been treated in such a way. *In no way does the method seek to induce a sense of shame or guilt.* At the same time, it is made clear to the suspected bully that there will be another meeting, and an arrangement for this is made.

It will be clear from this example that the success of the method depends upon the practitioner developing a positive and trusting relationship with the suspected bully. If the practitioner and the suspected bully have already been in conflict and any hostility has developed between them, the intervention is unlikely to be successful. Another practitioner will be needed.

Certainly much depends on the interpersonal skills of the practitioner in working with individual students – and also on recalling accurately what has happened during the meeting and what has been agreed to. It is tempting to take notes during the interviews, but doing so may well cause students to suspect that the practitioner is collecting evidence that could be used against them. It is best *not* to do so. Sometimes it has been suggested that there be two staff members present, one to interact with the suspected bully and the other to record what is being said. This is generally a mistake, as it involves staff outnumbering the suspected bully and can appear threatening. Under such circumstances the suspected bully is not likely to be so forthcoming.

As successive members of the suspected bullying group are interviewed, the practitioner develops a deeper understanding of the motives, attitudes and relationships that have influenced what has happened to the target. This understanding will be invaluable in working towards a solution. It may become increasingly clear that some members are more influential than others. Some members are more concerned. Some may remain obdurate; others have become more sympathetic to the victim. Some are more ready than others to resolve the issue. By interacting with the practitioner in one-on-one meetings, they are much *less* likely to maintain a mob mentality. Each student has, to some degree, become individualised. And this is an important achievement. They will henceforth be more ready to think for themselves rather than go with the tide.

The more successful the practitioner has been in eliciting constructive suggestions, the greater is the temptation to stop at this point. In fact, some advisers on the use of the method actually do indicate that the practitioner may stop here – and assume that the problem has been solved. This is often mistaken. There is more work to be done before the practitioner can feel confident that the bullying will not continue.

Meeting with the target

After all the suspected bullies have been interviewed, the next step is to interview the target.

In some cases, this will be the first time the practitioner and the target have met, or the first time there has been any discussion with the target about being bullied. As in the case of the meetings with individual suspected bullies, the practitioner should begin by explaining his or her role: to help students feel safe at the school and to help with any related problems. The practitioner can mention what he or she has heard about the way the student has been treated. Normally the student will confirm that he or she is having a hard time with some fellow students, and welcome the practitioner's help. The student's attitude towards the proffered help is likely to become more positive when it becomes clear that:

- there is no intention of punishing anyone, and
- meetings with the suspected bullies have taken place and they have indicated a readiness to help in solving the problem.

As stated earlier, the practitioner may have met previously with the target and possibly the target's parents. In this case he or she will have already indicated a readiness to help. At this second meeting, the practitioner provides an account of what has taken place in the meantime.

Again it is necessary to hold the interview in a quiet place where there will be no interruptions.

Occasionally, I have found that the target is sceptical about the practitioner's ability to stop the bullying. This is most likely to occur if the target has become very discouraged or depressed, and especially if he or she has sought help in the past and the outcome has been disappointing. In such cases, the practitioner must seek to provide reassurance. This can usually be done by emphasising that the suspected bullies have actually undertaken to make things better at meetings that have *already taken place.* On hearing this, the student is normally ready to talk about what has been happening. If not, the practitioner may need to spend some time exploring with the target how he or she feels about other students at the school. They may discuss together what are the good times and the bad times of life at school, especially with peers. Sooner or later, the practitioner will begin to learn how the target views others at school and what sorts of unpleasant things have happened while interacting with other students. This oblique approach may be necessary with some targeted students.

Once the target has opened up, what does the practitioner actually want to know? First, and most obviously, what the suspected bullies are actually doing that the target finds distressing. Second, the practitioner wants to know why the student thinks they are acting as they do. The target may, of course, be mistaken about the suspected bullies' motives, but it is useful for the practitioner to know what he or she thinks is the case.

As the student talks – and the practitioner listens carefully – a picture emerges of the kind of person he or she is. Questions form in the practitioner's mind about possible reasons for the bullying. Is the bullying entirely, or almost entirely, due to the prejudices or malign intentions of the suspected bullies? Are there features of the target's behaviour that seem to elicit the bullying? Is the target behaving in a socially unintelligent way? For instance, does he or she:

- show insensitivity to the feelings of others?
- continually intrude upon others without being asked to do so?
- look down on others, or boast about being more able or successful or socially superior?
- speak in an unnecessarily loud or pompous manner?
- neglect personal hygiene?

These are features the practitioner may think can be changed.

Some other features may not be so remediable. Here I have in mind autistic behaviour, Asperger and Tourette syndromes, attention deficit disorder, intellectual impairment, sensory deficits such as partial blindness or deafness. Children who are affected in these ways may elicit bullying behaviour from ignorant and unsympathetic peers. Although responsibility for their suffering rests heavily on the children who bully them, it may nevertheless be possible by skilful counselling and advice to reduce the likelihood that they will be bullied.

The practitioner may, however, come to believe that the bullying may be provoked by the victim, who is doing something deliberately to annoy or antagonise the suspected bullies. These students are often referred to as 'provocative victims', or even as 'bully–victims'. For example, they may have engaged in verbally abusing or spreading rumours about students who belong to racial minority groups or students who are thought to be gay. When those who have been thus abused – and become understandably annoyed – join together to 'bully' a provocative victim, a difficult situation arises. The bullying, however justified it may at first have seemed, must stop; but the provocative victims must clearly change their behaviour too.

Finally, there is the vast majority of victims who are in no sense provocative. They are sometimes called classical victims or innocent victims. Nevertheless, their 'innocence' needs to be inquired into. Hence, each time a target is interviewed, at some stage, typically after he or she has talked about the motives of the bullies, the question must be asked whether he or she may be doing something to bring on the behaviour (see figure 8).

Figure 8 Practitioner and targeted student: 'Tom, I wonder if there is anything you might be doing to cause them to treat you badly.'

Some students will immediately deny the possibility. The question could then be put more subtly: 'Do you think the bullies might *think* you are doing something to annoy them?' Here, of course, the implication is that the bullies may be misguided. But in answering this question the target is likely to begin to think about his or her behaviour more objectively.

In pursuing this line of questioning the practitioner must certainly avoid any suggestion that the target is to blame and deserves to be bullied. On no account should the target be put on the defensive to the point where he or she loses confidence in the practitioner.

The practitioner should always bear in mind the direction in which the Method of Shared Concern is taking everyone. Eventually there will be a meeting involving all the suspected bullies and the victim. At that stage the practitioner needs to have a good understanding of how the target views what has happened and his or her attitudes towards the suspected bullies. Importantly, the target will have to be prepared for that meeting.

The preparation can begin during this first interview. After reflecting upon his or her behaviour (with prompting from the practitioner), the target may be more aware of what contribution he or she could have made to the problem – and ideas may form as to how a solution might emerge. Moreover, the target can now be expected to feel more confident about a successful outcome, especially as trust in the practitioner's help continues to grow.

Before concluding this interview, a further reassurance is needed. It is made clear to the target that no meeting will take place which includes the target and the suspected bullies until the suspected bullies have actually demonstrated a sincere desire to find a solution.

Possible difficulties

It is not always easy to convince the target that one can help. The practitioner should not feel discouraged if the target is pessimistic about the possibility of a successful solution. Often students who have been victimised in the past have not been helped by those who have sought to help them. Targeted students may feel like hopeless cases. They may feel that the bullies are more powerful than the teachers, or that the bullies can continue to bully without the teachers knowing about it.

Throughout, the practitioner must remain empathic and supportive. This too may not be easy. The practitioner may feel that the target really is partly to blame. Earlier I mentioned a case of bullying of a primary school student who was being mercilessly hounded and bullied by several other students. Once it had been learned that the target had been engaging continually in racially vilifying the bullies (who came from a minority ethnic group) it became more difficult to feel empathy and concern for the target. Yet any loss of concern for the wellbeing of the target would have jeopardised the whole process.

Finally, there can be a sense of irritation with children who are victimised and do not act or react in a sensible way to help themselves. They may enter areas where they are much more at risk, rather than avoid places where there is some danger and where they have no need to go. They may overreact to teasing when other children good-humouredly shrug it off. Again the practitioner must avoid being judgemental, seek to understand why the target acts that way and patiently suggest ways in which he or she may best protect him- or herself, always bearing in mind that those who bully have no right to take advantage of such a person, and must learn not to do so.

In the example that follows the practitioner is meeting with the target for the first time, after being informed by some teachers that he is being bullied. The suspected bullies have already been interviewed individually.

Example: Interview with a target

T is a rather small, sensitive boy of 13. When he comes into P's office, his demeanour suggests that he is worried and unsure what to expect.

P: Good day. Please come in and sit down here. Just want to have a chat with you. Nothing to worry about. *[The greeting is warm and friendly, designed to put T at ease.*] Now, my role in the school is to help students feel safe when they are at school. I've heard that maybe you have been having a hard time with some of the other students lately.

T [*hesitantly*]: Yeah.

P: Would you like to talk to me about it?

T: Do I have to?

P: No, you don't have to. It's entirely up to you.

T [*earnestly*]: Will anybody get punished?

P: No, we are just trying to see if we can help in some way to make the situation better for you. [*P waits a while as T considers what to say.*]

T: Well, there's these three kids who go around together. They keep getting on to me, pushing me around, calling me names. They keep following me around. I can't go anywhere without them having a go at me ...

P [*sympathetically*]: Well, that must be pretty upsetting. I wonder why they are doing it. What do you think?

T: I don't know. [*Pauses, then angrily*]: I think they are just ignorant thugs. They are stupid. Sometimes I think it's because they are just no-hopers. Don't know what to do with themselves. They talk in an ignorant way. They don't know anything.

P [*thoughtfully*]: I wonder if there is anything you might be doing that causes them to treat you badly.

T: No, I try to have nothing to do with them.

P [*tries again*]: But maybe they think you are doing something that annoys them

T: I don't know. Maybe they think I am superior, but I'm not. Well, maybe I am in some ways. I mean they are really hopeless in their schoolwork. They are supposed to be good at football. But what's that!

P: I see. It's possible they think you're looking down on them.

T: And they keep going on and on about me being gay, but I'm not.

P: Well, that would be wrong, even if you were gay. They have no right to treat you in that way. [*Pauses.*] Have you any ideas about what you might do to stop them?

T [*dejectedly*]: Seems hopeless. I've tried to avoid them, but I can't. I've tried to reason with them, but they can't reason. I told my Dad and he just said insult them back. I tried that. But it was useless because there are three of them and they just laugh and it makes matters worse. I don't know what to do.

P: Now I wonder. Are they all the same or are some worse than others?

T: Well, Frank, he's the worst one. He's the ringleader. He eggs everyone on. He's a horrible, foul-mouthed person.

P: What about the others?

T: Well, there's Rose. She's Frank's girlfriend. She thinks he can't do anything wrong. Always laughs along with him.

P: Anyone else?

T: One of them, Phillip, isn't always that bad. He's brighter than the others. Sometimes I think he may not want to go along with them.

P: That's very interesting. Now let me tell you something. I have already spoken to each one of them. And, do you know, each of them appreciates that you have become upset and have agreed to help, if they can, to improve matters.

T [*looks dubious*]

P: And it may be you can help too. Keep your eyes open to see if there is any change in their behaviour towards you. You and I will be meeting again in a day or two and then I would like to arrange for you to meet with the group of students who have been bullying you.

T [*looks apprehensive*]

P [*picking up on T's reaction*]: Don't worry. I will not invite you to join them until they have shown a sincere desire to find a solution to the problem. And I will be there to support you. In the meantime, keep a lookout for how they might be changing their behaviour – and think about how you might be able to help them to change their behaviour by the way you behave. If we work together I think we might be able to solve this problem. Thanks. See you later.

Commentary

What has P learned from this interaction with T?

- It is evident that **T is being victimised** and is very unhappy about it. He is clearly not an 'imaginary victim'. Occasionally a student may pose as a victim to get other students into trouble, or may even misperceive the situation. In this scenario this is not the case. T is feeling quite miserable, and even that the situation is pretty hopeless. He needs help.
- **T is responding in a helpful way**, by describing in some detail what has been happening to him.

- **P has gained a useful picture of how T sees the SBs**, and especially that he is able to differentiate between the group members, recognising who is the ringleader and who may in fact be a somewhat reluctant follower.
- **P has discovered a clue to what may in some way be contributing to the bullying**; namely, T's sense of superiority, even arrogance, which may well have become clear to the SBs and provided them with some sort of justification for their attacks. Rather than confront T on how he might be provoking the bullying, P has raised a possibility in T's mind that he may well go away and think about it. A confrontation with T could result in him losing confidence in P.
- By revealing that he has spoken with the SBs, and that they have indicated a readiness to assist in solving the problem, **P has given T some grounds for optimism**.
- **P has informed T of the meeting with the SBs to which he will eventually be invited**, and for which he will need to be prepared. Recognising that attending such a meeting could be daunting, P has reassured T that no meeting will take place until the SBs have demonstrated that they really want to see the bullying ended.
- **T has been encouraged to think that there are good prospects of a successful end to the bullying**, but that he, T, will need to play his part.

This is, of course, only one possible scenario. In many cases there is little if any behaviour on the target's part that may need to be changed. Nevertheless, whether the target is an 'innocent' or a 'provocative' victim, some guidance may be needed in preparing him or her for the final meeting.

How the interview proceeds may differ somewhat if the target's parents reported the bullying to the practitioner before the meeting with the individual suspected bullies took place. In this case, the practitioner must separate what is learned from the student during the interview from what has been said by the parent. Interpretation of events may differ. Bear in mind too that the practitioner is concerned primarily with the target's perceptions rather than the 'facts' as others may see them. The practitioner is working with the target to bring about a satisfactory and lasting solution to the problem, not a considered judgement of who is to blame.

Checking on progress

The next step is to meet up with each of the suspected bullies again to see whether they have actually done what they said they would do to help to improve the situation for the target. Sufficient time must elapse to allow the suspected bullies the opportunity to carry out their expressed intentions. A day, or two, or three – but normally not longer – may pass before each suspected bully is seen again. The meetings may be fortuitous or as previously arranged, but again they should be conducted in a place where there will be no interruptions or distractions. They can be quite short.

In some cases students give convincing accounts of what they have undertaken. Sometimes a suspected bully may state that he or she has not yet had any contact with the target, but intends to do so. The practitioner may then point out that shortly there is going to be a meeting of all the students who have undertaken to help, and each of them will be asked to say what he or she has done and with what result. It is counterproductive to demand why the suspected bully has not already fulfilled a promise. (This does sometimes occur, together with a threat that 'there will be consequences if you do not do as you promised'. Clearly this is inconsistent with the spirit and philosophy of the Method of Shared Concern. But old habits sometimes die hard.)

These follow-up meetings are very important. Sometimes it is necessary to talk with a suspected bully more than once. Unless and until there is credible evidence that the suspected bullies have taken some action to try to improve the situation for the target, no further progress can be made. The Method of Shared Concern will need to be abandoned and an alternative approach adopted. Fortunately this very rarely happens. If the initial interviews with the suspected bullies have been conducted along the lines indicated and positive actions *have already been taken* by members of the group, it becomes possible to hold a group meeting with all the suspected bullies present. It can be anticipated that at this group meeting attitudes towards the target will be more constructive.[8]

The group can then be prepared for the last stage of the process, at which the problem will be finally resolved.

Endnotes

1. This training resource provides two role plays, with a commentary by Ken Rigby, illustrating how the method can be implemented, first with boys, then with girls. See Readymade Productions (2007).
2. Employing an approach to overcome bullying in Australian schools known as Shared Responsibility, Findley (2006) advocates the use of group meetings in all but the most recalcitrant of cases.
3. In the Support Group Method (see chapter 5) as proposed by Robinson and Maines (2008) the targeted student is interviewed first.
4. See Rigby and Barnes (2002) for estimations of percentages of students informing teachers after they had been bullied at school and a discussion of the difficulties students have in 'telling.'
5. Meeting with students identified as having bullied someone and teaching them about bullying and its consequences is a feature of a no-blame approach proposed by Findley (2006).
6. This extract from the writings of Soren Kierkegaard is excellent advice on the importance of non-judgemental listening as a crucial element in the application of the Method of Shared Concern. See Bretall (1973), pp. 333–334.
7. Lieutenant Columbo, protagonist of the television series Columbo which ran through the 1970s and beyond, was a seemingly slow-witted police officer who never sought to impress his suspects, treated them with the utmost respect, listened carefully to what they had to say – and invariably solved the case. See <http://www.legendarytv.com/columbo/index.asp>.
8. The view that taking action, especially if it is not induced through strong external pressure, frequently leads to relevant attitude change is a central feature of the highly influential theory of cognitive dissonance proposed by Festinger (1957).

Chapter 4 Working with groups

Exponents of the Method of Shared Concern claim that it is especially important to recognise the pivotal role of groups in accounting for bullying behaviour. This being so, it is *essential* that practitioners encounter the groups, for to a large extent they give rise to and sustain the bullying.

This of course is not a unique claim. For generations teachers have sought to resolve behavioural problems by targeting and addressing groups of students whom they felt were responsible for some wrongdoing. Here is a trivial and somewhat farcical example from my own schooldays. It began during a lesson in mathematics being taken by the principal of a secondary school I attended. Someone had let loose an offensive smell which soon permeated the room. The principal stopped the lesson and asked who had done it. Silence. He persisted. Students began to titter. Normally unruffled (an excellent teacher of arithmetic), he became furious. Nobody would admit anything. We were duly released at playtime, with the earnest expectation, if not the command, that the culprit would confess. The effect of this nonsense was, as you might guess, immense enjoyment on the part of the boys, a great sense of togetherness, and an almost infinite distancing from the infuriated principal. Oddly enough, the thing happened again a week later during a divinity lesson. The reverend taking the lesson sniffed the air and asked rhetorically: 'Who's farted?'

Farcical though the story is, it illustrates two things that are relevant to addressing bullying. One is that getting into a rage and threatening to punish a group is generally futile. The second is that when a teacher confronts a group of students who have done something wrong (however trivial) and accuses them en masse and requires a confession as a step towards resolving a problem, it is almost certainly doomed to failure, more especially with older students. And yet this continues to be done.

As we have seen, sometimes groups of bullies are convened by practitioners of 'no blame' approaches without any preliminary contact with the individual group members.[1] It is thought that confronting a group of students and seeking to sort out a problem with them will save time. I recall one practitioner of the Method of Shared Concern beginning with a group meeting of the suspected bullies, believing that the bullying was not a particularly serious case and could be resolved speedily. The result was a minor disaster. The students closed ranks. They refused to listen and would not cooperate. Adopting the correct approach subsequently by seeing each of them individually and gaining their cooperation became very difficult.[2] If the practitioner begins with a group interview the application of the method is apt to be both very frustrating – and time-consuming!

Meeting with the group of suspected bullies

Let us assume that sufficient evidence has been gathered from each of the suspected bullies – and possibly from others who have observed what has been happening – to convince the practitioner that a meeting of all these students as a group would now be helpful. A meeting is then convened at a time that is convenient for everyone.

What does the practitioner hope to achieve at this meeting? There are three connected goals:

1. the creation of an **atmosphere** in which the suspected bullies feel happy and relaxed and prepared to act together so as to bring the conflict between them and the target to an end
2. the provision of an opportunity for each member of the group to take part in developing **an agreed and credible plan** to bring about a satisfactory outcome for both themselves and the target

3. an understanding among the suspected bullies of **how they can apply that plan** in a practical and effective manner in their subsequent interactions with the target.

Creating a congenial atmosphere requires some preparation. Again the meeting place should be one where there will be no interruptions or distractions. Ideally it should be a place where students feel comfortable; away from the bustle and noise of corridors; certainly not a classroom with rows of desks. Pikas has suggested that the suspected bullies should be treated like special guests and provided with food and drink. In Australia I have found that teachers find this suggestion unacceptable. Perhaps in some cultures it would be otherwise. But anything that can be done to help the students feel welcome is to be commended.

How the suspected bullies are welcomed is crucial. Each is addressed by name and treated as an acquaintance. The meeting can begin with the practitioner congratulating everyone on their helpful actions in seeking to resolve the problem. Each student may then be asked to describe what he or she has done, and with what outcome. Some may report that their efforts to bring about a change in their relationship with the target were unsuccessful. The target may have been 'unreachable', or even rude. Every sincerely made, positive contribution should be recognised and reinforced. What matters is not the success of the effort but that it was made, and that others could learn from it.

The question naturally arises as to what the group will do next. The obvious answer – commonly suggested by the students themselves – is that they must meet with the target. If they do not make this suggestion then the practitioner must do so, and gain their acceptance.

Appraising the group situation

In listening to what the group members have to say, the practitioner discovers how they feel about the current situation. What happens next will depend on the appraisal the practitioner makes of their readiness to negotiate a positive outcome with the student they had targeted. Here are some possibilities:

- **The group as a whole is sincerely committed to helping the target to feel better.** They are sorry for how they have behaved. They want to make up for what they have done. There has been, it seems, a change of heart. They are even ready to offer the hand of friendship. All this seems to augur well for a happy ending. But will this euphoria be sustained? What will happen when they meet the student they have been bullying? The target may not be all that enthusiastic about receiving their apologies and expressions of goodwill. Trust is not easily re-established. The group may be in for a disappointment.

- **The group feel that they want the episode to end, but they do not want to be friends.** They cannot manufacture any warm feelings towards the target. They feel nothing, or perhaps a vague dislike. But they recognise that the school is in earnest about stopping the bullying, and they are prepared to acquiesce. They may see it as in their interest to leave the target alone. Some, if not all, may be glad to see the bullying stopped. They may actually dislike the culture of bullying in which they are enmeshed, principally because they could become victims themselves. It may now have dawned upon them that there are better things to do than go around bullying other people. Here we see the change in the behaviour of the group motivated more by an enlightened self-interest than by a sense of empathy. There is no way this group is going to be best buddies with the target. The practitioner may feel disappointed, having hoped for a more compassionate outcome. But the central aim of the intervention, to bring about a condition of safety for the target, is nonetheless being achieved.
- **The group may still harbour feelings of resentment towards the student they have targeted, and perhaps even towards practitioner.** They are unwilling to admit to themselves that they were in the wrong, or wholly in the wrong. They may feel – despite the non-blaming attitude of the practitioner – that somehow their case for treating the target with contempt has not been properly appreciated.

  Here the skill of the practitioner may be tested. At the end of the day, how can it be ensured that there are no winners and losers?
- **The practitioner may recognise that the group of suspected bullies has relatively little 'togetherness'.** They disagree among themselves about what should happen next, with some seemingly sorry for what they have

done, some angry, some unrepentant. It is not unusual for the process of Shared Concern to bring about or bring to the surface such individual differences, and this may even be seen as a healthy development. Members are beginning to think for themselves. But it does put demands upon the practitioner, who must now help the group to reach a consensus as to how they are to proceed in their coming meeting with the target.

Making a plan

The plan is worked out before the final meeting with the target to achieve the objective of resolving the problem and bringing about a sustainable discontinuation of the bullying to the satisfaction of all concerned. It must clearly take into account the motivations and intentions of the suspected bullies; all of them, if possible.

This aspect of the Method of Shared Concern is crucial. Unfortunately, it is sometimes not undertaken adequately, sometimes not at all. Every member of the group of suspected bullies should be involved. Every proposal must be considered; every misgiving entertained and respected. Only when there is a general agreement about what is to be said to the target can a final or 'summit' meeting be called.

The *process* of achieving the plan is of great importance. It is tempting at times to impose a 'solution' on the group, one that the practitioner feels will be in the best interest of everybody. But it is wiser to call for suggestions or proposals from group members and to examine each one dispassionately, allowing everyone to make comments. This may take time.

In some cases the plan may be relatively easy to reach agreement on, as when everyone feels a need to apologise and act in a friendly, restorative manner; although here the practitioner may seek to sensitise the students as to how the target might feel about their *volte face*. The target may not in fact quite believe them.

Where there is no desire on the part of the group to acknowledge remorse or to act in a friendly manner, the practitioner may feel inclined to *exhort* them to be nice to the target. This can be a mistake. Recognise that it is an important step forward if the students simply make it clear that they will not continue the bullying. Yes, it would certainly be nice if they were all genuinely positive, but one cannot dictate how people must feel. The suspected bullies may well think:

The feelings I don't have I don't have.
The feelings I don't have, I won't say I have.[3]

At the same time, unless the suspected bullies deliver their message to the target with respect it is unlikely that there will be a permanent or sustainable cessation of hostilities.

Where there is a residual sense of resentment and suspicion, the practitioner needs to proceed very cautiously. As we have already seen, sometimes victims do behave provocatively. Often they don't, but may be thought to have done so. Students who bully others are prone to rationalise; that is, to attribute their own actions to creditable motives and dismiss more obvious and plausible explanations for their behaviour which everyone else can plainly see. Whatever the reasons the suspected bullies may give for their reluctance to act positively towards the target, they should be taken seriously. The practitioner needs to know where they are coming from; failing this any subsequent mediation between the suspected bullies and the victim is not likely to succeed. Any plan must address the misgivings that the suspected bullies may have. But it must be a credible plan: one that the target can accept.

Where there are significant differences among the suspected bullies, some discussion in the group may be facilitated to reconcile divergent points of view. This may not be easy. As members of the group interact there can be shifts in power and influence. Alliances of students with agreed positions may form. The ringleader may find that he or she can no longer lead; may in fact become a target! It is in this somewhat fluid situation that the practitioner must seek a common ground that can be accommodated in an agreed plan.

The practitioner must ask the group to come up with an agreed plan about how they will proceed at the next meeting, which will be held with the target present. They will need to formulate what is to be said to the target on behalf of the group – and also anticipate the target's reactions. The plan must be practicable, one that has a good chance of bringing about an end to the bullying that satisfies both the suspected bullies and the target. The practitioner provides the group with the opportunity there and then to formulate, discuss and come up with a plan (see figure 9).

Figure 9 Practitioner and a group of suspected bullies: 'I would like us now to make a plan for when we meet with Tom.'

The emerging plan may take different forms, according to the wishes of the group. It may range from an olive branch approach to a tough negotiating approach. It will need to accommodate all the members' basic concerns. But there are some givens: the plan must be directed towards bringing an end to the bullying, and the plan must have a good chance of being acceptable to the target.

Importantly, the plan must be presented in such a way as to maximise its chances of success. This means that each side must treat the other with respect, which – given the history of conflict and suspicion between the parties – is much easier said than done. The practitioner's role is to make this possible.

Careful preparation of the group for the meeting with the target is essential. Here are my suggestions:

- **Ensure that everyone is clear about the plan that they have agreed to.** If misunderstandings and arguments break out among the suspected bullies when they meet with the target, there is reduced chance of success.
- **Have the group recognise that the target is likely to feel threatened and anxious at the meeting, and will need to be reassured of their goodwill.** Ask them to think about what each can say to put the target more at ease when he or she joins them at the next meeting. It is useful to have them briefly rehearse what they will say in front of other members of the group.
- **Decide how the joint plan is to be presented.** This commonly involves a representative from the group stating what, as a group, they have agreed to say to the target as a means of resolving the problem.

- **Get the group to try to anticipate how the target will respond when the plan is presented, and how they might be obliged to negotiate.** The plan is not to be seen as a take-it-or-leave-it affair.
- **Have the group acknowledge that they just might see the situation differently after they have heard what the target has to say.**
- **Make it clear that the meeting will not be a contest about who is right or who will win,** but rather an opportunity to make things better for everyone.

Only when this preparation has been completed should the target be invited to join the group in a further meeting.

Inviting the target to join the group

Once it has been agreed by the group that the target is to be invited to join them to finally resolve the problem, the practitioner must communicate the news. Typically, a brief meeting takes place between the practitioner and the target at which the outcome of the meeting with the suspected bullies is described. It can be explained that the group are well intentioned. They sincerely want to resolve the problem once and for all. For that reason they want to talk with the target, with the practitioner present. The target is assured that the practitioner will be supportive at the meeting and enable those present to reach a solution that is acceptable to everybody – to the suspected bullies, to the school and to the target above all. If a positive and trusting relationship with the practitioner has developed, the student will normally be prepared to come along.

There may, however, be cases in which the target is reluctant to come to such a meeting. Recently I encountered a case handled by the Method of Shared Concern involving the sexual harassment of a girl by two teenage boys. They had deliberately sought to embarrass her by continually suggesting that she kept staring at a place on one of the boy's trousers covering his penis. When she denied that this was the case, they laughed and repeated the suggestion. She was deeply embarrassed, angry and unable to think of a way of handling the situation. The case eventually came to the attention of a practitioner of the Method of Shared Concern. Following individual meetings with each of the boys and then with the two together, it became clear that they understood the distress that they had caused and wished to improve the situation. They discussed how this could be done and sought to have a meeting with the girl in the presence of the practitioner, when they would sincerely apologise. Not entirely surprisingly, the girl declined the invitation. Although she recognised that the boys were sincere – they had already acted positively to bring about respectful relations with her – she was not prepared to be reminded again of the embarrassing and humiliating episode. The practitioner decided that she should not be pressured to come to the meeting, and the boys were told about her decision. Although a more public reconciliation would have been helpful, it was considered more important to respect the girl's wishes.

In nearly all cases the target agrees to come along, feeling confident that there will be a good outcome to the meeting. But some preparation with the target may be undertaken, especially if it is thought that some hard negotiation with the suspected bullies will take place. This is likely to occur when the target has, to some degree, provoked the bullying – or is seen by the suspected bullies to have done so.

The practitioner may discuss with the target what concessions he or she is prepared to make in the interest of getting a good outcome. For example, if the target has said some unkind or offensive things about the suspected bullies, then it would be helpful to acknowledge that this has happened and is regrettable. If the target has in the past adopted a superior and disdainful attitude towards the suspected bullies, it would be a good idea for the target to act at the meeting in a respectful manner towards them, even acknowledging some positive things about them, especially if they are prepared to reciprocate. It may be useful to rehearse with the target how to respond to what the suspected bullies might say.

Making concessions may seem reasonable enough when the target has been provocative and has (perhaps without realising it at the time) been insensitive in dealing with suspected bullies. But when the target is innocent, or largely innocent, making concessions is harder to justify. The target may feel particularly annoyed at having to admit to 'provocations' that were not intentional – or were possibly a figment of the suspected bullies' imaginations.

There are two things that may be said when this difficulty arises. First, concessions can be made more easily if they do not reflect badly in any significant way on the target's character. For instance, a person may admit to laughing on one occasion because something happened that seemed funny (as in someone slipping on a banana skin), without realising that to the other person the resulting injury was not funny at all. Second, there is the conditional apology: 'I'm really sorry if you were offended by what I did.' The utility – and acceptability – of such responses in some situations should be discussed with the target.

At the same time, however well planned the response of the suspected bullies might have been – and whatever the practitioner might think about its adequacy – the target must be satisfied that the proposal that has been made is sincere, fair and acceptable. There can be no *a priori* guarantee of the acceptability of a proposal. What happens at the meeting will in part depend upon the goodwill and social intelligence of the students present, and, of course, on the social skill of the practitioner.

The summit meeting

The final meeting should follow soon after the meeting between the suspected bullies and the practitioner. In part, this is because with the passage of time the suspected bullies may forget their commitments, or come to think they were mistaken in making them. Further interactions may have occurred with each other and with the target, and these may alter their attitudes and resolution to fulfil their promises. Also, if the practitioner takes too long in convening a final meeting, the suspected bullies may actually decide to resolve the matter themselves by holding a meeting with the target without the practitioner being present. This happened in a recent case in which the method was being applied.[4] Although this showed initiative, in the absence of the guiding influence of the practitioner further disputes and conflicts arose among group members and resulted in an unsatisfactory outcome.

The summit meeting provides an opportunity for the suspected bullies, the target and the practitioner to come together to resolve the problem on which they have been working for the past few days. It must be a joint effort. But first the practitioner should take stock of what has been achieved already and what outcomes are possible.

- **The practitioner will have got to know each of the suspected bullies through the series of one-to-one meetings, and now sees them as individuals in a group with distinct personalities, motives and attitudes.** They may have unique perceptions of their friends, and also of the target. Each suspected bully has been treated with respect. None of them has been threatened by the practitioner. In some cases, if not all, a degree of empathy for the target has been aroused. Some will have been questioning whether their behaviour towards the target has been fair. At the same time, the practitioner may have discovered among some of the suspected bullies a resentment towards the target, especially if he or she has behaved provocatively. It is likely that some will be torn between loyalty to the group and sympathy for the target. Some may wish the group to which they belong – and to which their self-esteem is attached – were somehow different, perhaps less threatening to them personally.
- **The practitioner has some knowledge of what individual suspected bullies have actually done, following the initial meeting, to help to resolve the problem.** This may be taken as an indication of a genuine desire to bring about a new, positive relationship with the target – or (possibly) a response to the subtle persuasiveness of the practitioner. In either case, any positive acts can be taken as a good omen.
- **The practitioner has established a relationship with the group.** He or she now has first-hand knowledge of how they interact together, and understands just how cohesive or otherwise they are as a group. Although there may be some differences in opinion among members, it has become possible to see how the suspected bullies as a group feel about the target, and what they are prepared to do.
- **The practitioner has now seen a credible plan emerge from discussions within the group;** importantly one for which there is group support and which has a good chance of success.

Intended outcomes

What outcomes are now possible? It is always wise to have goals in mind before the meeting begins. Basic goals are:

- most obviously, the **discontinuation** of the bullying

- the **establishment of acceptable relations** between the suspected bullies and the target
- the **sustainability** of the acceptable relations.

One may – and should – aim higher. One would like them all to be good friends with the target. But in many cases this is unrealistic. Even among people who admire and have goodwill towards each other there is no guarantee that they will always be 'friends.' In the Method of Shared Concern the basic concern is with the psychological safety of the target. Whatever may be added is a bonus.

Sustainability is clearly important. When bad relations have existed between people for a time, it is not surprising that old animosities sometimes revive. In applying the Method of Shared Concern we seek to reduce the likelihood that this will happen.

At the summit meeting

It should be arranged for the suspected bullies to meet with the practitioner once again for a little while, about 10 minutes, before the target is due to join them. This is to prepare for what is to come, and especially for the suspected bullies and the practitioner to recall what they had agreed to do and say when they interact with the target.

It is important that the suspected bullies should be clear about the part they are to play. They are expected to greet the target personally when he or she arrives, recognising that he or she may feel anxious in meeting with those who may have earlier behaved in a hostile and threatening way. Further, each is expected to have something positive to say directly to the target. The meeting will be unlikely to succeed if the target is given a cold reception. But the way suspected bullies behave should not be forced; for if it is, the target will find it inauthentic. We should bear in mind that the target may well be sceptical about the good intentions of the suspected bullies.

The group are further prepared for the meeting by re-acquainting them with what they have agreed is to be said to the target to resolve the conflict and dispel the bad feeling that has arisen. The spokesperson should rehearse what he or she is going to say on behalf of the group. They are reminded that the target may have things to say to which they will need to respond –

and that they should do so thoughtfully to bring about an agreed solution to the problem

Finally, the practitioner may ask them to agree to certain rules as to how they will behave when statements or opinions are expressed with which they disagree. Instructions may include:

- **Listen** carefully to what is being said.
- Treat everyone with **respect**, even if you do not agree with them.
- **Don't talk over** other people.
- Remember that everyone has agreed that they want to re-establish and maintain **good relations** with the target.

As planned, when the target enters the room, he or she is greeted by the practitioner and by each suspected bully, and seated next to the practitioner. When asked by the practitioner, each suspected bully in turn makes a positive and credible statement about the target. Then the practitioner asks the spokesperson for the group to make a statement on behalf of the group, and asks the target to reply.

The suspected bullies meet with the innocent victim

The suspected bullies have planned to say they have agreed to stop bullying the target. Their statement may or may not be accompanied by expressions of regret or remorse. They may, or may not, say that they want to be friends with the target. They may say no more than that they intend to leave the target alone and offer reassurances, as in figure 10.

Figure 10 At the summit meeting: 'Don't worry, mate. We'll make sure it doesn't happen again.'

The suspected bullies will have been prepared by the practitioner to expect that the target might be suspicious of their motives and doubt their sincerity. That is why they may have made it very clear that the bullying is well and truly over. But if the target is unimpressed, it is hardly surprising. The suspected bullies may need to be reminded that in the past they have treated the target badly, and it can't be easy for him or her to be forgiving.

The target is certainly not pressured by the practitioner to be forgiving, but may be counselled (beforehand) to accept any apologies or offers of goodwill gracefully – in the interest of improving relationships and ensuring his or her safety. The practitioner may (tactfully) praise both the suspected bullies for their good sense in agreeing to discontinue the bullying, and the target for accepting that they are acting in good faith.

It is nonetheless a good idea to remind the students that in all relationships between people things can go wrong, and they should be prepared to talk to each other or seek help if there is any recurrence of bullying behaviour. The practitioner must express a readiness to be available to help.

The suspected bullies meet with the provocative victim

In this case the role of the practitioner is much more demanding. There is tension in the air, no matter how much planning has been done. The suspected bullies have agreed that they will seek to bring about an end to the conflict. They have a carefully conceived plan. They are going to say that they will not continue to bully the target any more – but they still feel resentful. Yes, they have acted disproportionately to the provocation. They have gone too far. But, damn it all, the target was not entirely blameless. The target must also accept some responsibility – or so they believe.

As with the innocent victim, the suspected bullies have nevertheless agreed to the rules and promised to act respectfully. They are ready to begin by saying positive things about the target. Then the spokesperson will convey their carefully prepared statement – or offer – and await the target's reply. The practitioner must now mediate. The following is an example of what might happen.

Example: A summit meeting with a provocative victim

Four SBs had been interviewed by P: Jenny, Jessica, Jean and Jane. Each had acknowledged that Joanne (T) had been having a hard time. Somewhat reluctantly at times, each of them had undertaken to help P make things better for her. In follow-up interviews it was apparent that the SBs who had had the opportunity to do so had made some effort, not always appreciated by Joanne, to act more positively towards her. They reported that they had smiled and said hello to her in a not unfriendly manner, and one of them had had a few words with the ringleader of the group and suggested that she could stop being nasty to her.

Meanwhile P had interviewed Joanne, who was clearly still upset by the way she had been treated. It transpired that Joanne had at one stage been a member of the group that was now bullying her. Some weeks ago she had quarrelled with two of the group members and had sought to discredit them by spreading stories about how mean they had been to her. Seemingly as a consequence, she had been receiving unpleasant text messages. She suspected that these were coming from some of the group members. When she approached them they laughed and turned their backs on her. Despite the general unpleasantness of her ex-friends Joanne still felt that it would be nice if they accepted her again, and at times she had tried to join them. On each occasion they were rude and rejecting. Now she felt very much alone and without friends. In the interview with P it was evident that Joanne was angry and distressed by what had happened, but recognised that she may have contributed in some small measure to their hostility.

When the SBs gathered for the summit meeting they were told that Joanne would be joining them in about 10 minutes; but first they had to go over what they had decided to do when she arrived.

P: Good to see you all again. [*Greets everyone by name.*] This is our final meeting. Let's make it a good one. Joanne will be joining us soon. But first let us recall what we decided we would say to her [*pauses while the SBs think about it*].

Jane: I think we said that we would all greet her. Yes, and say something positive about her.

P: That's right. What was it you were going to say, Jenny?

Jenny: I was going to say that I really appreciated the way she helped me with my geometry last term.

P: Is that so? I think that will help her to feel valued in some way. Remember she is going to feel a bit anxious meeting with all of you again. How about you, Jean?

Jean: I found this really hard, because she has been very nasty to me. But I have thought about it and I am going to say: 'You know, Joanne, we had some good times together once.' That's all.

P: That's good. You can say that sincerely, can't you? [Jean nods.] How about you, Jessica?

Jessica: I'm a bit like Jean. Joanne hasn't been nice to me either. I'm just going to say: 'Glad you've come along'.

P: OK. That's fine. Now Jane?

Jane: I thought I would say that I thought she was brave to come along to talk with us today. It couldn't have been easy.

P: That's true. Well done, all of you. Now let us recall the proposal that you are going to make to Joanne.

It had been decided that Jessica was going to be the spokesperson. They listen carefully to what she is going to say, and agree that it sounds right. When they have concluded, P rises, goes outside where Joanne has been waiting and brings her in.

P: Thank you very much for coming, Joanne. Please sit down. [Joanne takes a seat next to P.] I believe you know everybody here. Each of them would like to say something to you.

Each of the girls, first Jane, then Jean, then Jenny and finally Jessica, say hello and then add what they have prepared to say.

This has broken the ice, but there is still a feeling of uncertainty as to how things will develop.

P: Now, Joanne, they have been talking with me about what we can do to help improve their relationships with you – and, as you know, things have been pretty bad over the last few weeks. Jessica is going to tell you what they think can be done about it.

Jessica: Joanne, we have had a good talk together, and we are sorry you've been upset by the way we've been treating you. But, you know, you haven't been very nice to us – and we know you've been saying horrible things to others about us, especially Jean. So we didn't want to have anything to do you with and …

Joanne [*interrupting*]: You didn't have to send me those nasty text messages!

P: Wait a minute! [*Speaking to all the SBs.*] What are you going to say about that?

Jenny: Well, we shouldn't have done that.

Figure 11 At the summit meeting: 'We are sorry, Joanne, but you haven't been very nice to us, you know.'

Joanne: Thanks, Jenny.

Jessica [*continues*]: Well, this is the way it is. We won't say or do anything more to upset you. And you, we hope, will not try to make trouble for us.

P [*turning to Joanne*]: Are you happy with that?

Joanne [*pauses for a while*]: Well, I can't say I'm really happy – but I am glad you've said that there won't be any more unpleasantness from you. I'm sorry too if you thought I was being mean about you all. I was just upset, that's all, and felt I had to tell people why.

Jessica: Well, I think we can understand that.

At this point P felt that acceptable relations between the students had been achieved. There was no evidence at this meeting that they would be friends again. There was still the chance that they would not sustain their improved relationship. So the P needed to talk with the SBs further about the need to keep in touch with each other, not necessarily as friends with Joanna, and be ready to recognise any signs that the conflict could begin again – and, if there were signs, to talk to each other about the situation. P thanked everyone personally for their efforts in helping to resolve the problem and said that she would be happy to talk with them again if they wanted to see her to discuss the matter further.

Some issues

Sometimes the target is not the best judge of what concessions are reasonable. The target should not be permitted to leave the meeting thinking that he or she has conceded too much, and has been too weak or compliant. Under such circumstances the target's self-esteem will suffer. The target may suspect that the 'bullies' are laughing about her. If that seems quite possible, the practitioner may intervene by asking the group to consider whether making a particular demand on the target was fair.

On the other hand, an impasse may develop if the target refuses to accept any suggestion that he or she may have acted in a way, consciously or unconsciously, to bring on the bullying. Here the practitioner may seek to restrain suspected bullies from reacting angrily and remind the target that a person can, at times, give offence without meaning to do so.

Once the suspected bullies and the target have reached an agreement about how they should henceforth behave towards each other, it is sometimes too hastily assumed that that is the end of the matter. It may not be so. Outside the meeting room with no practitioner to guide them there could be times when the provocation and the bullying start again. The Method of Shared Concern seeks to address this possibility.

The question must be raised as to how the agreement that has been reached is to be sustained. It is sometimes raised by one of the suspected bullies or by the target. It is likely that at this stage all or most of the group members will want the bullying to end for good. After all, that is what they have been working towards. But they may well recognise that the conflict might start all over again. If none of the group members acknowledges this possibility the practitioner should raise the question: What can be done to ensure that things don't go wrong again?

Various answers may be suggested. It might be hoped that with the experience the group has had of non-punitive problem-solving, no-one will suggest that anyone who breaks their promises will be punished. But some do! One can, however, *generally* rely upon support in the group for a more understanding or tolerant approach.

There are two things the practitioner can do:

1. **Convince the students of the utility of keeping open channels of communication between the suspected bullies and the erstwhile target.** This is especially important when it has been decided that the relationship between the students is going to be a somewhat distant one: a live and let live arrangement. Suspicion of each other is likely to grow if they do not communicate, even if the communications are no more than an occasional 'hi!' Suspected bullies can be convinced that it is in their interest to speak up when they see trouble coming – trouble they want to avoid. The target will understand this too. Neither side will want to blunder blindly into a further conflict. As Pikas has suggested, an early warning system is of much benefit to both sides.
2. **Produce a contract which sets out clearly in words agreed upon by the students what they have promised to do.** Once this has been worked out to everyone's satisfaction, all those involved in the meeting add their signature. This becomes a document that may be consulted and invoked if there are indications that the students are ignoring or forgetting their commitments.

Neither a communication contract (an agreement to discuss any concerns that arise before they get too big), nor a contract that sets out a formal agreement are guarantees that the bullying will never recur. The most influential factor will be the learning experience of the students in taking part in the Method of Shared Concern.

We could leave it at that – and that's where it is often left. As we shall see, to a remarkable degree the method works. But undoubtedly it works better as the practitioner acquires a deeper understanding and corresponding skills. We can learn best when we keep a record of what we did and what the outcomes were. For this reason, it is proposed that the practitioner keeps an account of what happens during each implementation of the Method of Shared Concern (see Appendix 1 for a pro-forma that can help in this process). This record should seek to identify where the practitioner might have gone wrong as well as where he or she went right. In time it becomes possible to identify with increasing reliability the cases for which the method was most appropriate, as well as the difficulties that were experienced.

If this method is going to catch on and be used most effectively, it will do so largely through the efforts of those teachers and counsellors who critically assess both the method, and themselves as users of the method. They can become leaders who transform the way many cases of bullying are humanely and effectively and permanently handled in schools.

A summary of the process

In this and the preceding chapter I examined in detail what is done by practitioners of the Method of Shared Concern, and occasionally I have examined and discussed reasons that have been proposed to justify what is done. This focus on the detail means it is quite possible that the wood is at times lost among the trees. It may therefore be useful to conclude this part of the book with a brief summary of the steps that are taken in applying the method.

It is important to grasp the process of applying the Method of Shared Concern as a whole. The stages fit together through a logical process as follows:

1. **Information leading to the identification of a case of bullying suitable for an intervention using the method is derived** through reports and

observations that, as far as possible, do not involve the target in disclosing the identities of the bullies.

2. **Persons identified as suspected bullies are interviewed individually.** Concern over the plight of the person who has been targeted is shared with each suspected bully, who is then invited to suggest possible solutions to the problem and make a commitment to assist.
3. **The targeted student is next interviewed and offered support.** The target's situation is explored, and the possibility of the bullying being to some extent provoked is considered.
4. **Brief meetings are held with each of the suspected bullies** separately to monitor progress and, if this is considered adequate, a group meeting with all the suspected bullies is convened.
5. At the group meeting, **the suspected bullies are prepared for the final or summit meeting with the target.** They are asked to make a plan or proposal which they will subsequently share with the target.
6. At the summit meeting they are joined by the target, and **a solution to the problem is negotiated.**

Endnotes

1. See Findley (2006).
2. This case is described in a report commissioned by the Australian Department of Education, Employment and Workplace Relations (Rigby & Griffiths, 2010). The report is available at http://www.deewr.gov.au/Schooling/NationalSafeSchools/Documents/covertBullyReports/MethodOFSharedConcern.pdf
3. These two lines are taken from a poem by D H Lawrence: 'To women as far as I am concerned.'
4. See Rigby and Griffiths (2010).

Part 3 Evaluating and introducing the Method of Shared Concern

After we have learnt how the Method of Shared Concern is supposed to work, we are left with two related questions. These are:

1. **What is the evidence that it really does work?** Unless there is a positive and convincing answer to this question, there will surely be no point in introducing this radical way of handling school bullying. A school community needs to be convinced that the method works before it can approve the steps needed to bring the method to the school.
2. **What needs to be done if the evidence favouring the use of the method is persuasive?** How can the Method of Shared Concern be best introduced to a school?

Chapter 5 provides an appraisal of the method, first by stating and then critically examining the beliefs and assumptions underlying its use, drawing upon relevant social and psychological theory where this is available. It then looks at the research evidence relating to its effectiveness in resolving bully/victim problems. Finally, it compares the Method of Shared Concern with other approaches to bullying, noting strengths, limitations and areas in which each may be best applied.

Chapter 6 addresses the question of what schools need to do if they decide to introduce the method. What are the practical steps that need to be taken to ensure that the introduction is acceptable to the school community and that the method is applied with the best chances of success?

Finally, in chapter 7 I have suggested how the Method of Shared Concern can be introduced into professional development sessions as part of in-service training. In this I have drawn upon my own experience of doing so in a number of countries, including Australia, England, Singapore, Hong Kong, Ireland and the United States. Details relating to suggested role plays are provided in appendix 2.

Chapter 5 Appraising the Method of Shared Concern

In appraising the approach taken by practitioners of the Method of Shared Concern, I want to try to answer the following questions:

- What do practitioners of the method actually **believe** – and are their beliefs reasonable?
- What is the **evidence** for suggesting that the Method of Shared Concern is an effective approach?
- How does the Method of Shared Concern **compare** with other intervention approaches?

Beliefs of the practitioners

The most basic belief of practitioners of the Method of Shared Concern can be summed up in an old saying:

'All children between the ages of one and one hundred years adopt an idea if they discover it as their own.'[1]

Hence the general aim of the practitioner is to bring about the conditions in which those involved in bully/victim problems spontaneously form the conviction that they must work towards a constructive solution. This idea must be their own. These conditions cannot involve coercion of any kind – not threats and punishment, or the deliberate inducement of shame, or the use of peer pressure.

The practitioner further believes that the locus of motivation to engage in bullying is not to be found exclusively in either the individual or in the group to which the individual belongs. It involves both. Hence the practitioner must work at the individual level and also at the group level to achieve a satisfactory and sustainable outcome.

The practitioner believes that a solution to the problem requires the employment of a number of stages:

1. **initial one-to-one interviews with suspected bullies** in which there are no threats or punishments. These serve to *individualise* each of them and gain their unforced cooperation
2. **a meeting with the target** to offer support and gain an understanding of the part he or she may have played in what has happened
3. **monitoring the subsequent actions** undertaken by each of the suspected bullies
4. **convening a meeting of the suspected bullies** after constructive actions have been taken by each of them towards a solution. At this meeting a plan is made to share with the target, who is then invited to join them
5. **a final meeting with the suspected bullies and the target** to reach a final and sustainable solution.

The practitioner also believes that *each* of these stages is necessary in dealing with bully/victim problems of a non-criminal nature in which there is group involvement.

As well as noting the beliefs of the practitioners, it is important to acknowledge what they do *not* believe.

They do not believe that students who bully are individually not responsible for their actions. They *are* responsible. The method seeks to bring about a commitment to responsible action. Further, they do not believe that every student who engages in bullying does so for the same reason, or quits for the same reason. Some students may bully because of personality reasons, some because of group pressure, some for a combination of these reasons. Some quit because they have begun to empathise with the target, some because of feelings of remorse, some want the bullying to stop because they may be the next target. Some do so because they have learned that there is indeed a better way of behaving. But in all cases the outcome is seen as a consequence of an educational process leading to an unforced decision to act to bring the bullying to an end.

Are these beliefs reasonable?

The answer will depend in part on personal judgements and assumptions made about the attitudes and behaviours of students who become involved in bully/victim problems at school. For instance:

- Is it reasonable to assume that young people are commonly enmeshed in the modus operandi of their friendship group?
- Does interacting with a group member *alone* enable the practitioner to make a personal contact and share a concern for a targeted person that would be difficult or impossible when addressing the group as a whole?
- Does making a contact in this way help to detach the student in some degree from the group influence and in a sense *individualise* that person?

Experience suggests that for each of these questions the answer is 'yes.'

At first blush the idea that a bully will respond empathically to an account of the distress of a person he or she has helped to target may appear counterintuitive. We are accustomed to thinking of the stereotypical bully as devoid of empathy. Research does not, however, confirm this belief. The average level of affective empathy (but not cognitive empathy) found among students who have been identified as frequently engaging in bullying behaviour is somewhat lower than that of others[2], but the difference is small, and in a one-to-one situation with a non-accusatory practitioner the suspected bully is generally ready to acknowledge the sad plight of the target and undertake to help in some way.

Can the target be expected to welcome an offer of help from the practitioner? Given that he or she is commonly in a desperate situation, and the practitioner is able to point towards some real progress after speaking with suspected bullies, the answer is likely to be 'yes'. But will the help be acceptable when the practitioner raises the question of whether the target has in some way contributed to the problem? Here it depends how the question is raised. The utmost tact is clearly needed.

Is it really necessary to ask this question? Given that in a significant proportion of cases some degree of provocation on the part of the target has taken place, it is clearly reasonable to discover whether the target has in some way provoked the bullying.

Earlier it was noted that progress could best be made with individual suspected bullies by detaching them from their group for a one-to-one talk with the practitioner. Could bringing them together later be risky? Could it resurrect the mob mentality? Arguably not, if each person has actually undertaken to do something to improve the situation for the target – and this is a precondition for holding such a meeting. And not if they as a group can agree to work together on a plan to complete what each of them has begun. What may have been a negative peer influence at the start (to be avoided) can become a positive peer influence at the end. One might reasonably expect the group and its members to feel collectively empowered.

Can the target be expected to join them? Yes, if convincing assurances have been given, and, most importantly, the target has already experienced some changes in the way he or she is being treated. Is the final or summit meeting really necessary? This question will be answered more fully later, but here it may be noted that it is all too easy to delude oneself into thinking that a conflict has been resolved and then discover that it was only a temporary pause in hostilities. The reasonable practitioner will take steps to ensure as far as possible that the solution is sustainable, especially when a provocative victim has been part of the problem.

Finally, let us return to the primary belief of practitioners of the Method of Shared Concern: that an idea will be accepted when it is discovered as one's own. The essence of the approach is to bring about an unforced realisation that it really is in the interest of each group member to work towards an acceptable and sustainable solution. Whether this is achievable requires an examination of the evidence from an evaluation of how the method works in practice. This we will do presently. But first it is useful to examine an alternative view of what is happening when the Method of Shared Concern is applied.

The practitioner and the suspected bully: An alternative view

Practitioners of the Method of Shared Concern see themselves as agents of change largely through their indirect influence on the motivations of individuals and groups involved in bullying. But it has been argued that the practitioner may bring about change in another way. This alternative view assumes that the trouble with bullies is that they have a history of unsatisfactory relationships with adults, often starting with feelings of non-acceptance in their own families.

There is some evidence that supports this view.[3] A rejection of adult authority may lead to an intense preoccupation with gaining support from a peer or friendship group, and a rigid conformity with the norms of such a group. For such students, forming a positive relationship with an adult can be a new experience, highly significant for any future development.[4] This can happen if the practitioner behaves in a genuinely supportive and non-judgemental way. One consequence may be a weakening of reliance on the peer group and a readiness to accept values different from theirs. It may result in the acceptance of more mature and traditional (adult) values that endorse respect for the dignity of individuals – values that are incompatible with bullying.

This explanation for the success of the Method of Shared Concern is not inconsistent with a view that emphasises changes brought about by practitioners in the dynamics of groups. Arguably, it may account for changes in the behaviour of some children who bully, especially those whose bullying behaviour is related to insecurities derived from a history of negative relationships in the home.

There are nevertheless dangers in assuming that all or even most bullying is related to inadequate relations with adults. Granted, secure attachment to caregivers, especially at an early age, is a factor in making possible subsequent positive relations with peers, as studies have shown.[5] But many children whose relations with parents are positive still bully. It is also misleading to assume that the weakening of peer influence on a child is invariably desirable. Obviously it depends on the peers. While recognising that some children who bully can be helped by developing a positive relationship with a mature adult, proponents of the Method of Shared Concern also recognise that as children develop, the peer group – especially friendship groups – inevitably become more and more important relative to parents, and it is vital to work *with* friendship groups rather than against them. This is what the Method of Shared Concern attempts to do.

How effective is the Method of Shared Concern?

It is all very well, it might be said, to discourse on what is reasonable or theoretically sound, but of prime concern is whether the method actually works; that is, whether there are empirical grounds for supposing that its application results in an improvement in the situation of those who are being targeted, and a cessation or reduction in the practice of bullying. Estimation of the effectiveness of the Method of Shared Concern has been undertaken in a number of ways.

One way is simply to note how widely it has been adopted. There is good evidence that it has been considered acceptable as an intervention method in anti-bullying programs in a range of countries including Spain, Scotland, England, Finland and Australia.[6] But how well has it been regarded by teachers when it has been used?

One systematic investigation has been reported in England.[7] Teachers in schools where it was being applied were asked to rate its effectiveness in dealing with cases of bullying. Altogether teachers from 155 schools across England rated its effectiveness on a five-point scale from 1 (not at all satisfied) to 5 (extremely satisfied). The average rating was 3.9, which is well above the midpoint on the scale. This suggests that teachers in England where it is being employed generally approve of its use. But we should bear in mind that having adopted the method it is unlikely that users would produce judgements that were at variance with what they had decided to do.

Students are less biased judges of its effectiveness. The method was used in a secondary school in New South Wales, Australia, as part of an anti-bullying program which significantly reduced peer victimisation in year 7. Students reported very positively on the contribution that the method had made in reducing the bullying.[8]

Where the effectiveness of applications in specific cases of bullying has been estimated, the results appear highly supportive. Studies conducted in secondary schools in Sheffield, England, revealed that reductions in bullying were reported by three out of four students with whom the method had been applied, and that five of the six teachers responsible for employing the method claimed that it had reduced the frequency and severity of the bullying.[9]

A study in Scotland reported that the method was applied successfully or very successfully in 34 out of 38 cases among children aged 7–16 years.[10] Reports in Western Australia from trained school personnel/school psychologists using the method indicated success rates of 85–100 per cent in upper primary and secondary schools.[11] In each of these studies the success or otherwise of the applications was assessed by the practitioner, arguably not the most neutral of raters.

Ideally, outcomes from applications of the method should be assessed by someone other than the practitioner, who can be suspected of bias. In the nationally funded study in Australia the application of the method in 17 cases of bullying in schools in Tasmania, Victoria, South Australia and Western Australia included interviews with all the participants, conducted individually by neutral investigators.[12] Positive changes were reported in 15 of the 17 cases; some were more positive than others. In general, both the suspected bullies and the targets reported that the situation had much improved.

Of particular interest to the researchers were reports from those who had been targeted. In two cases, targeted students were not accessible, having left the school. Twelve of the reports indicated that the bullying had stopped. Examples of the targets' comments included:

- I was not bothered and their teasing stopped.
- They stopped talking nasty and started talking nice – treated me like a friend.
- Great. They don't do the big bullying any more. It makes me feel better not putting up with the bullies.
- They stopped calling me names and picking on me.
- [Things are] pretty good, better than I thought it would be.

There were three cases in which the targeted students indicated that their situation had definitely improved but were uncertain whether the bullying had really ended. Further follow-ups were needed.

Although the focus must be primarily on outcomes for the targeted individuals, the method seeks to bring about changes in the thinking and behaviour of the bullies as well. In practically all the post-intervention interviews with the suspected bullies there was evidence that they felt they had benefited personally from their involvement. Here are some examples of their recorded comments:

- The meetings helped me to stop and think.
- Looking back I felt bad about bullying.
- Judith looked happier because we all said nice stuff.
- We stopped giving him a hard time and apologised for our behaviour.
- It was good, because we are kinder to Phyllis and not teasing her any more.
- We are going to be finishing year 7 soon and when we look back on primary school, we want to have happy memories and for her to feel OK and us to feel good about ourselves.
- I'm happy for myself because I've been helping people and helping him to feel better about himself.
- Good, me realising how much I was doing it; John feels better, so do I.

With few exceptions, the suspected bullies were positive about having taken part in the process. Some were enthusiastic:

- I enjoyed the process, as I didn't feel as though I was going to be punished for my actions.
- Both sides of the story were heard and it was possible to speak freely.
- I think because of these meetings it has improved the friendships John has made.

Findings were clearly supportive of the method's effectiveness in a large majority of cases. If we compare the outcomes with what students generally report happening after going to a teacher for help, the approach is clearly vindicated. Recall (from the Introduction) that approximately 50 per cent of students who tell a teacher they are being bullied do not report any improvement at all, and 10 per cent or so report that things got worse.

Why, it may be asked, was the method not entirely successful?

An examination of the cases that produced the least positive outcomes suggests possible reasons. In one case, the practitioner thought she could begin by interviewing the students in a group. This only strengthened their resistance to being 'empowered'. In another case, there was a high degree of provocation due to the target having racially abused and spread malicious rumours about the students who eventually initiated and sustained the bullying – with the support of community members outside the school. We should bear in mind, too, that some of the practitioners were relatively inexperienced in using the method and can be expected to improve with practice.

The final reason can be summed up simply by saying that dealing effectively with cases of bullying can be really hard. Every case can be quite different – and the challenges they offer to some extent unpredictable. Applying the Method of Shared Concern is as much an art as a science.

The range of applicability of the method

There has been, as yet, little exploration of the range of problems to which the method can be successfully applied. Generally it is assumed that it is most relevant to problems that involve groups of adolescent students who are engaged in bullying one of their peers. It is worth noting, however, that in the study described above[13] four of the 17 cases involved primary school students, and in three of them the outcomes were positive. In one case the target who was being bullied by adolescent students was not a peer but a teacher who was accompanying a group of students on an excursion from school. The teacher sought the assistance of the school counsellor, who successfully applied the Method of Shared Concern to bring about a highly satisfying solution to the problem.

It has been suggested that the method can be applied to cases of cyberbullying when the perpetrators have been identified.[14] Another case from the study involved two adolescent girls who had posted highly defamatory and offensive information about another girl on a site created to enable people who are angry about something or somebody to let off steam. The girl's parents became aware of the targeting (it was described in a local newspaper). At first they wanted to have the offenders, who had in fact been identified, suspended, but eventually agreed that the issue be negotiated through the Method of Shared Concern. The two girls acknowledged the distress they had caused, and a solution acceptable to all parties was reached. While behaviour verging on the criminal may appropriately be dealt with using a traditional disciplinary approach, in some circumstances a better outcome, one that avoids rancour and thoughts of revenge, can be achieved through a sensitive application of the method.

There is then evidence that the method can be used effectively with cases differing in terms of the ages of the students involved, the nature of the offence and the role of the target; that is, whether a fellow student or a teacher. The approach is more robust than had been supposed.

Comparison with other approaches

In making appraisals of a particular approach to dealing with cases of bullying it is sensible to consider how it compares with alternative approaches. Few books have set out to make comparisons of this kind.[15]

However, when comparisons are made it is evident that each has strengths and limitations and may be suitable for use in one kind of situation but not another. Here is a summary of my attempt to compare the Method of Shared Concern with five other major approaches.

The traditional disciplinary approach

As noted earlier, this approach has the advantage of being supported by a high proportion of teachers in a range of countries, with around three teachers in four believing that it is an appropriate way of dealing with low-level severity cases of bullying. As a result it is generally easy to reach agreement among teachers about using this approach to deal with a case. This makes a whole school approach more feasible. Parents too tend to support this approach, especially when their children have been bullied at school. It is seen as administering justice, and as likely to send a message to other students about what will happen to them if they engage in bullying. It appears relatively straightforward. Rules against bullying are devised and publicised. The facts relating to the case are identified and the school delivers a punishment that fits the crime. The bullies are deterred from further bullying, and so are those who observe what has happened to them.[16]

Unfortunately it is not quite so simple. Some educators see bullying as far too complex to be nicely encompassed by 'rules'. For example, students can be seriously damaged by continual isolation and exclusion. Collecting all the evidence relating to what has happened to someone and why it has occurred can be far from straightforward. It can be both time-consuming and demanding.

The kinds of punishments that are available to teachers, including suspensions, are often not sufficient to deter. Given the comfort those who bully commonly get from their supporters, the paltry sanctions imposed on them by the school may have little effect. The bullying may become less conspicuous by going underground, but be just as damaging to the target.

In fact, despite its popularity in many schools, evidence for the effectiveness of this approach is mixed. Early reports of the success of the Olweus program[17], which is highly supportive of the disciplinary approach (albeit accompanied by sustained educational initiatives in classrooms), have generally not been replicated outside Norway.[18]

Monitoring the effects of such treatment on those who have bullied can be difficult and time-consuming. The saving of time in using the traditional disciplinary approach rather than the Method of Shared Concern may be illusory. Certainly if the Method of Shared Concern does produce a sustainable change of heart in the suspected bully, time spent in monitoring the situation becomes unnecessary. At the same time, there are, as suggested earlier, some cases in which a disciplinary approach is needed, especially if the victim and other students are at serious risk and their protection can only be achieved by denying the perpetrator the opportunity to hurt them; and this can be difficult.

Strengthening the victim

If the victim can be strengthened sufficiently to repel the bully this is a great achievement. The bullying stops, the victim recovers any lost self-esteem (indeed, self-esteem may go through the roof) and of course the school is relieved of the need to take action. As noted earlier, developing the necessary skills is never easy. However, there are victimised or potentially victimised students who need to learn how to act in an assertive and socially intelligent way so that they are no longer bullied.

The problem here is twofold:

1. **Identifying students who are being bullied and are capable of acquiring the necessary skills to protect or defend themselves.** In some cases, it may be obvious that the victimised student *cannot* be made safe without someone intervening to change the bully's behaviour. The odds may be such that the

victim cannot prevail by personal effort, either because the perpetrators are too powerful or the victim is too handicapped. In other cases it is not unreasonable to help the targeted students to acquire both the confidence and the social skills to cope more effectively, especially with unpleasant verbal teasing or taunting; for example, through the employment of a 'fogging' technique which helps the bullied student to act assertively, focusing upon the perceptions of the bully rather than the validity of what the bully is saying.[19]

2. **Finding someone with the skills and time to work with the victim to produce the necessary changes in the capacity to resist the bullying.** This can be quite time-consuming. Changing submissive patterns of behaviour in some victims can be very difficult, and may require the skills of a trained psychologist.

We may conclude that strengthening the victim is an important and desirable aim, but its achievement is limited to cases in which it is realistic to expect the victim to acquire the necessary skills even with guidance from a committed helper. Unlike the Method of Shared Concern, it is not concerned with bringing about sustainable changes in attitude on the part of those involved in bully/victim problems. It is not concerned with improving relationships between children, but rather with equalising power so that some children will escape being hurt by their peers. One may well ask whether power differences between children, as between adults, can ever be eliminated. There is arguably more hope in seeking to help people see that it is in their best interests in a good society not to abuse their power.

Mediation

This approach has been staunchly supported by some school educators who have provided instruction and guidance on how it can be applied.[20] In some schools it is applied by trained peer mediators. When it is successful, the consequences can be highly beneficial not only to the students whose dispute has been resolved, but also to the school community as it sets an example of how interpersonal conflicts can be solved amicably without the use of force. It can also benefit the peer mediator, whose social competence and self-esteem are greatly enhanced.

On the other hand, the proportion of bully/victim cases that can be addressed through peer mediation is quite limited. Both the suspected bully and the victim must be willing, without any compulsion, to be mediated. The suspected bully is often reluctant to come to the meeting. He or she can generally see little benefit in doing so. Further, the mediator must be prepared to act in a neutral and even-handed manner, favouring neither side. In cases of bullying this is often difficult to justify. The practitioner is apt to feel that the suspected bully is in the wrong and needs to change, certainly more so than the victim. Not only may there be an unwillingness on the part of a possible mediator to be neutral, but it is often the case that there are few teachers or students who have been appropriately trained for the task.

Thus although there are great benefits to individuals and to schools in bringing about a mediated solution to a dispute, the opportunities for mediation to be applied in cases of bullying are few and far between. A positive outcome is likely only under conditions in which:

- there is a minimal imbalance of power between two students who are in conflict
- both students want to see an end to their conflict
- a trained mediator is available; and
- the mediator can act in a neutral manner.

It may be observed that the Method of Shared Concern may also involve a degree of mediation. That is true – but only after a considerable amount of work has been done with individuals and groups to prepare for its success.

Restorative practice

This approach has become increasingly popular in recent years, and is currently being used in many schools.[21] It is appealing because it promises to avoid the negative features of the traditional disciplinary approach, while at the same time bringing about a just resolution of problems involving offensive behaviour.

Different applications of the approach have been devised to deal with problems of varying severity in which individuals or groups are involved. For instance, restorative practices are sometimes employed to resolve conflicts between two individuals, as well as conflicts among members of a class of students. In cases of severe bullying, restorative practices may be applied in 'community conferences', which include members of the wider community such as parents. Central to its justification is the belief that offenders ought to feel remorse for what they have done, and should be brought to recognise their responsibility for the harm the victim has suffered. It turns out that many children who bully do experience a sense of remorse when they are confronted with evidence of the consequences of their actions, and are ready to apologise and repair the relationship they have damaged.

There are several limitations to this approach:

- It is not effective in cases of bullying in which the offenders do not experience remorse despite the efforts of the practitioner to induce that state of mind.
- The approach does not take into account the fact that there are sometimes two sides to a story: the suspected bully's and the victim's. The bully is branded the offender. The innocence of the victim is thereby assumed. While this is often a reflection of reality, it is not always so. As we have seen, some victims are indeed 'provocative'.
- The process is a 'blaming' one. However we spin, the prisoner is in the dock. The offender may agree to comply, may indeed be contrite, but the decision to turn over a new leaf has been achieved in some cases under duress, and one may speculate on whether it will last.

Restorative practice and the Method of Shared Concern are sometimes confused. They have in common a reaction against the traditional disciplinary manner insofar as it seeks to produce change through fear. They also share a desire to bring about a restoration of a relationship that has in some way been damaged. However, the differences are important. While the employment of restorative practice in cases in which a bully has evidenced sincere remorse is sensible and often relatively quick, there are many cases in which a more in-depth approach is justified. These typically require the unforced cooperation of a group of students who can be brought to see that it is in their interest to help bring about a solution to an acknowledged problem. With the Method of Shared Concern, solutions are negotiated rather than demanded.

The Support Group Method

In its philosophy this is the closest to the Method of Shared Concern. It assumes that the bullying to be addressed involves groups of students rather than isolated individuals.[22] It seeks to gain their cooperation by avoiding directly blaming them for their actions and by sharing with them a concern for the plight of the victim. At a group meeting they are asked how they can improve the situation in some way.

There are some important differences. In the Support Group Method the bullies are not interviewed individually, and at no stage does the victim attend a meeting with them. It is assumed that the victim is innocent of having provoked the bullying in any way. It also makes use of assistance from students who have not been involved in the bullying. Several students who are expected to be supportive of the victim attend a group meeting along with the bullies; this can provide some peer pressure on the bullies to act pro-socially. A notable advantage of this approach is that it can be carried out more quickly, without the practitioner becoming involved in a series of meetings with *both* individuals and groups.

There are several limitations to this approach:

- No attempt is made to explore the perspectives of the individual bullies prior to a group meeting. It is assumed that they are all more or less alike. In fact, they may have different motivations and have played different roles.
- No opportunity is given to group members under the guidance of the practitioner to plan how they as a group will negotiate a resolution of the problem with the victim. They can come to feel that they have been pressured to behave in an acceptable way by 'non-bullies' who have been specially brought into the group meeting for that purpose. Consequently their actions are less likely to be intrinsically motivated.
- Importantly, the Support Group Method takes it for granted that the victim has not acted provocatively and, moreover, does not need to be present at any stage in working out a solution to the problem with the bullies.

The claims of the Support Group Method cannot however be discounted; indeed, there is persuasive evidence of its effectiveness, especially from research conducted in England.[23]

In the majority of cases the victim is in fact innocent, and the influence of his or her supporters or sympathisers is clearly beneficent. However, in some cases it is desirable to explore the situation in greater depth by working first with individual suspected bullies and then, after progress has been made, with the suspected bullies as a group. With a greater understanding of the situation – and especially with the involvement of the suspected bullies in negotiating a resolution of the problem with the victim – a more sustainable outcome can be expected.

Discussion

It has been argued above that the set of beliefs held by practitioners of the Method of Shared Concern are reasonable and supported by evidence from social psychology. Especially it is thought that cases of bullying need to be addressed by taking into account the relationships that students who bully have with *their* friendship group. Such support is often crucial to the continuance of the bullying. It is also very clear that a hostile, accusing approach to students who bully is unlikely to lead to their cooperation and, as a consequence, a positive outcome for the victim of their aggression.

A major claim of the Method of Shared Concern is that it is more likely than other methods to ensure a safe outcome for victims. This is because the method can change the motivation of perpetrators and help to bring about a negotiated and sustainable end to the bullying. Unless the enmity between the bullies and the victim is somehow overcome, the bullying is likely to continue, commonly in covert ways, and protection of the victim is extremely difficult to achieve. The most important reason for intervening in cases of bullying is to bring about a situation in which the victim is safe.

An additional bonus is that there is a real chance that the application of the Method of Shared Concern can bring about a change of heart in the bullies (which will *not* occur when they are simply forced to comply) and result in those who have taken part in the bullying adopting more constructive ways in relating to others. Given the harm that is perpetrated by unreformed bullies, the benefits to society can be very great indeed.

Arguments rage about whether the prime focus of interventions should be on the victim or the bullies. The answer is that they should concern themselves with both. Often it is claimed, fairly enough, that interventions in cases of bullying in schools do just that. But unfortunately they do so, in my opinion, in the wrong way. Typically, the victim is counselled and the bullies are punished. The victim is comforted and/or strengthened and the bullies are reprimanded and subjected to a sanction, such as a detention. Not surprisingly the parties learn nothing or very little; perhaps the bullies may learn to bully covertly; generally the victim feels none the safer.

When the victim has been provocative, the school is commonly in a quandary. The victim must be made to admit to being provocative and be duly punished; the bully who strongly retaliates must also be punished. One can imagine them exchanging none too friendly glances as they sit silently in the detention room, having learned nothing. As against this dismal remedy for bullying, the Method of Shared Concern offers a prospect of social learning in the company of all those concerned.

A review of the evidence regarding the effectiveness of the Method of Shared Concern as an intervention method indicates that it has, in an increasing number of studies, achieved success, although further evaluative studies are still needed. This is in marked contrast to the paucity of evidence supporting most other methods of intervention. This does not mean that schools should not undertake to make their own appraisals of the effectiveness of the method in their own unique school environments. By carefully recording how faithfully and especially *in what circumstances* the Method of Shared Concern has been applied, and what the outcomes have been, schools can gain additional evidence of its effectiveness.[24]

Finally, in making an appraisal of the Method of Shared Concern schools should recognise the costs involved in its adoption. Bear in mind that it can be more time-consuming and require more specialised training than other methods. Comparisons with other approaches show that it is more thorough and comprehensive. But this does not mean that other approaches should be abandoned. These can sometimes (not always) be used in conjunction with the Method of Shared Concern; for example, techniques for strengthening the victim can be helpful in some circumstances. As noted earlier, there are times when other methods may be more appropriate, as when a traditional disciplinary approach is needed to deal with cases of violent bullying; or when restorative practice is used appropriately in cases in which an individual bully is genuinely remorseful; or when, without a shadow of a doubt, a victimised student is innocent and the Support Group Method is justified. What is needed in making a valid appraisal is an appreciation of what other methods have to offer and when it is in the best interest of students to employ them.

Endnotes

1. Quotation supplied by Pikas (personal communication).
2. In a study conducted with adolescent students in England, Jolliffe and Farrington (2006) reported that cognitive empathy – as in being able to appreciate another's distress – was unrelated to bullying behaviour. However, relatively low levels of affective empathy was found among both boys and girls who bullied frequently.
3. Negative relations with parents have been reported in several studies as being related to students engaging in bullying at school (Rigby, 1993; Baldry & Farrington, 2000; Rigby, Slee & Martin, 2007).
4. This view is strongly promoted by Neufield and Mate (2005), who argue that the mental and social wellbeing of children depends largely upon their being closely attached to a caring adult.
5. Troy and Sroufe (1987) were the first to demonstrate the long-term effects of inadequate attachment on a child's relationships with peers at school.
6. Descriptions of its application in these countries are given in Smith et al. (2004) (England); Duncan (1996) and Sullivan (2010) (Scotland); Ortega, Del Rey and Mora-Merchan (2004) (Spain); Salmivalli et al., (2004) (Finland) and Petersen and Rigby (1999) and Griffiths (2001) (Australia).
7. See Smith (2001).
8. See Petersen and Rigby (1999).
9. See Smith and Sharp (1994).
10. See Duncan (1996).
11. See Griffiths (2001).
12. See Rigby and Griffiths (2010). The cases in that study varied widely in both the gender and ages of the participants, and in the nature of the bullying that had taken place. Most of the cases were from lower secondary schools. Three were from upper primary and three from upper secondary schools. Two were from special or alternative schools that catered for students with behaviour problems. The cases included verbal, physical, sexual and cyberbullying.
13. Rigby & Griffiths (2010).
14. Counselling and intervention methods, including the Method of Shared Concern, that are considered appropriate for addressing cases of cyberbullying are described and examined at length in Bauman (2011).
15. One exception is *Bullying interventions in schools: six basic approaches* (Rigby, 2010b).

16. This approach is consistent with the most widely adopted anti-bullying program promoted by Olweus, Limber and Mihalic (1999), and employed extensively in schools in the United States.
17. See Olweus et al. (1999).
18. Attempts to replicate the success of the Olweus program as implemented in Norway have been unsuccessful in Germany and Belgium. See Smith, Pepler and Rigby (2004). A more recent study in middle schools in the United States in which the Olweus program was employed was found to have some 'mixed positive effects varying by gender, race/ ethnicity and grade, but no overall effect' (Bauer, Loranzo & Rivara, 2007, p. 266).
19. The technique of 'fogging' is described and illustrated with examples in Rigby (2010b).
20. See Cowie and Wallace (2000).
21. See Thorsborne and Vinegrad (2006).
22. See Robinson and Maines (2008), who together pioneered the Support Group Method
23. See Smith, Howard and Thompson (2007).
24. As discussed in Rigby (2010b).

Chapter 6 Bringing the Method of Shared Concern to a school

This chapter assumes that this book has somehow fallen into the hands of someone who now wants to see the method implemented in their school. How can it be done?

Here is my advice to teachers.

The first step is to make a realistic assessment of the method's acceptability. If you are new to a school you may well be in the dark. If you have been on the staff for some years perhaps you may have some idea. But not necessarily. Perhaps there has been little or no discussion of how cases are to be treated, or at least not when you have been present. Raise the matter cautiously with interested colleagues. Best not to sound like a true believer! Rather raise the matter as if it were out of mere curiosity.

You may find that some staff members are not open to your ideas, having decided upon one particular approach to dealing with problems. Statistically, this is likely to be the traditional disciplinary approach. If so, discuss the virtues of this approach – and any possible limitations or drawbacks.

Avoid promoting the Method of Shared Concern as an ideology. Never argue, for instance, that the use of punishment is intrinsically unacceptable as a means of resolving conflict, even if that is your opinion. You are likely to get further if the discussants are persuaded to look for themselves at the evidence for the effectiveness of particular approaches in dealing with bullying.

Here are some questions that may become relevant as a discussion about the viability of the traditional disciplinary method proceeds:

- When students are punished for bullying someone, does it generally act as a deterrent?
- Is it likely that the bullying may become more covert, go underground and inflict at least equal harm on the victim?
- Is it realistic for staff to monitor all, or even most, cases of bullying after students have been punished?
- How sure are we that we can be 'just' in using a punitive approach to bullying? Are there not cases in which the victim has in fact acted provocatively and is at least partly to blame?
- Under what circumstances does the law or agreed school rules require that a disciplinary or punitive approach be used?
- What alternatives to the traditional disciplinary approach might be considered?

Once staff members have begun to show a serious interest in these and related questions, you may suggest a session in which staff members complete the Handling Bullying Questionnaire (HBQ) (see appendix 3). Sharing answers to these questions is sure to produce surprises and lead to further discussion on what should or can be done. What will emerge is a more detailed picture than can be obtained through discussion of what the staff really think they should do when cases of bullying arise. The answers will reveal some useful information:

- What proportion of staff believe that a punitive approach is best, even in cases of relatively low-severity forms of bullying?
- How many – if any – feel that no action is really necessary; that students should 'sort it out' for themselves?
- How many feel that students can and should learn to 'stick up for themselves' – with (or without) help from others?
- How many believe that mediation between bullies and victims is a practicable strategy – and in what proportion of cases? And in what circumstances?
- How many think that parents should, or should not, be involved in dealing with cases of bullying? And with what kinds of bullying?

- How many think there should be persons on staff *identified* as being empowered to handle bullying cases, rather than leaving it to individual staff members?
- How many feel that students should be induced to feel remorse when they have bullied someone, along the lines indicated by proponents of restorative justice?
- How many believe that it is possible to work constructively with students who have engaged in bullying someone, without resorting to interrogation and overt blaming?

Answers to these questions can provide useful information about the way staff members are thinking, and their readiness to consider the possibility that the Method of Shared Concern could provide a viable means of addressing some cases of bullying.

Once there is genuine interest in the method, then and only then is it useful to explore the possibility of using it as an approach to *some* cases of bullying. It is unwise to urge it as a universal panacea. What is needed next is an accurate presentation of the method and its rationale. It is often useful to invite someone who has actually used the method successfully to talk to the staff and ask them to engage in role plays to understand the method better. Resources in the form of articles and DVDs can be helpful (see appendix 6).

In the course of discussing the Method of Shared Concern, questions typically arise as to how it differs from other methods that do not rely on punishment. Especially, staff are likely to want to know how the Method of Shared Concern differs from Restorative Practice and the Support Group Method (see pages 95–8). At some point the discussion will turn to the evidence for believing that the Method of Shared Concern can be effective. This should be provided and discussed (see chapter 5). Questions will inevitably arise about the time commitment that is needed in applying the method. The diagram suggesting a timeline in appendix 4 can be used to focus discussion. Finally staff will be interested in available training. Explore how this can be obtained by contacting experienced users (see appendix 6).

Students and curricula

To a large extent the success of the Method of Shared Concern depends on the beliefs, attitudes and social intelligence of students. In these respects there can be big variations between schools. Where there are more students at a school who have positive and well-developed social skills, the Method of Shared Concern is likely to be more effective.

In planning content for a school curriculum that addresses bullying, I suggest beginning with a review of what may be achieved through lessons and classroom activities that will result in students being *less* likely to be involved in bully/victim problems and *more* likely to act in ways that are helpful in the implementation of the method. It might then be asked what knowledge, beliefs, attitudes and skills can be induced, or strengthened, to help bring this about. Here is my list:

- knowledge of what bullying is and the forms it can take
- recognition of the harm bullying can do to individuals and to society
- acknowledgement of its unacceptability in a school
- realisation that everyone in a school has a *responsibility* to help in the prevention and the resolution of bully/victim problems
- attitudes that are socially sensitive, cooperative and inclusive
- the possession of social skills that enable students to form and maintain positive social relations with others, and provide practical assistance to those who are experiencing conflict.

The value of a universal approach

If we are to promote the Method of Shared Concern optimally, the school curriculum must include content and activities directed towards the development of the appropriate knowledge, attitudes and skills of *all* students. It may be argued that not all students are equally likely to become involved in bully/victim problems. This is so. Some students are indeed more aggressive, insensitive or vulnerable than others. But there are good reasons why a universal approach is needed.

- **Most, if not all, students can become involved in bully/victim problems under some circumstances.** For instance, they may be pressured by their friendship group to support the bullying of someone who is disliked by some influential members of the group. Individuals may become the target of group prejudice, regardless of their attitudes or social skills. Experience of working with groups of 'bullies' reveals that they sometimes include students whom one would never have expected to have bullied anyone.
- **If the Method of Shared Concern is going to work optimally it really needs the support of students in general; ideally, everyone.** This is much more likely to be achieved if there is a good understanding of what bullying is and the harm it can do, together with a sensitivity to others that ensures students will support the method and do so in a practical way, especially by informing teachers of those who can be helped by practitioners of the method.

This last point is crucial. It is well known that students are often averse to telling teachers about cases of bullying they observe.[1] To some extent, this is because students do not believe that teachers care enough or, if they do, are capable of helping. If teachers can actually demonstrate that they can help to resolve problems to the satisfaction of students, this difficulty can be overcome. Establishing a high level of trust is not easy, especially with adolescents, but at least movement in this direction is possible if teachers are seen to be in earnest about working with students to solve problems, and moreover can do so not by imposing a solution but through genuine collaboration. It is well to remember that most students hate bullying and would like to see an end to it.

Involving students

What then can schools do as part of their curricula to develop the conditions in which students are more likely to support the Method of Shared Concern, and, if they become part of the process when the method is applied, work effectively towards bringing about a sustainable solution? Here are my suggestions.[2]

First, students should be systematically taught about bullying in ways that are appropriate to their age group. They should learn about how bullying is defined, what forms it may take, its prevalence in schools and, above all, the harm it can do. Only when students are concerned about its harmfulness, as well as its unacceptability at the school, will they be motivated to act and support measures to reduce it.

Student support for countering bullying can more readily be obtained when students participate meaningfully in the development of the school's anti-bullying policy. Hence it is desirable to stimulate discussion among students in class about how the school can best tackle the problem. Elicit suggestions from them, and pass these on to those directly responsible for developing and articulating the policy. Students can also be asked to provide feedback on what is actually being proposed. They may see things that others miss. There is no doubt that the students will be sensitive to the issue of teachers bullying students!

Circle time

Anything that results in students becoming more sensitive to the feelings of others is helpful. One useful activity is *circle time*.[3] This involves bringing students together from time to time to participate in a meeting run by a teacher at which they can exchange views on matters that concern them personally. Such meetings need to be carefully prepared. Proceedings must be orderly, with clear rules about when it is a student's turn to speak. There is a requirement that speakers not be interrupted. Students are encouraged to talk about positive things as well as things that they might like to see changed. It is often wise to counsel members to speak only about matters they feel comfortable talking about. The leader of the group (normally a teacher) has a responsibility to help students steer clear of matters that are confidential. This may include problems with their family members and issues that need to be disclosed confidentially to authorities, such as cases of sexual abuse.

Circle time can have important consequences for how students feel and behave. If it is well conducted, students begin to gain some appreciation of how others feel. Typically they are pleasantly surprised to find that many feel as they do. They begin to see that despite some first impressions, students *are* generally sensitive and greatly concerned about what is happening to others – as well as to themselves.

Students are typically not aware that other students feel as they do. They are initially unaware that others too have finer feelings. Much of their energy goes into keeping up appearances, projecting a tough stoical image, to be like the others, or more accurately *to be like what they think the others are like*. Psychologists have called this misperception of the thoughts and feelings of others 'pluralistic ignorance'.[4] This can be dispelled once you give students the opportunity to talk openly and frankly about how they really feel.

Although circle time is not intended as a problem-solving exercise, it may prove helpful in that regard. Suggestions may be given by members of the group about how a student may learn to cope more effectively. It is not intended as a meeting at which bullies are to be identified, exposed and dealt with – although some students may become 'hot under the collar' if they hear someone talking about having experienced distress for which they are in some way responsible. It may have incidental therapeutic benefits for victims who realise that they are supported by at least some students – and a restraining effect on those who engage in bullying, as they begin to appreciate both the harm they might do, and also the widespread opposition to bullying behaviour being openly displayed by those responding sympathetically to what victims have to say. Finally, members of the circle may come to see that the teacher who is running the group is truly concerned about how they feel, and may be trusted to help those in need.

Cooperative learning

The successful operation of the Method of Shared Concern is also likely to be facilitated when schools are able to introduce cooperative learning as a means of improving the learning of school subjects.[5] The effects of participating in classroom activities that reward cooperativeness are especially important to students who tend to become involved in bully/victim problems. It has been shown that both bullies and victims are typically less inclined to cooperate than others.[6]

The Positive Peer Group Program

Cooperative activity is most in evidence when a group of people decide to undertake a project that they all want to take part in. How this can be brought about with groups of students, including disaffected youth, has been demonstrated through the use of a so-called Positive Peer Group Program.[7]

This program solicits from young people suggestions of 'worthy' school-based enterprises and then assists rather than directs them in implementing their suggestions, for example, painting the school's stairwell, crafting and installing a logo and signage for their school, visiting feeder schools to talk to children who will subsequently be attending their school and reassuring them that they will be made welcome when they arrive. Such activities are likely to increase both the capacity and the motivation for students to participate constructively as group members in planning to resolve bully/victim problems. This, it will be recalled, is a very important task that is tackled by some students in the penultimate stage of the Shared Concern process.

Inculcating positive values

Much has been said about the centrality of positive values in addressing bullying in schools. Clearly a student may know *how* to be sensitive to others and how to cooperate with them in addressing a problem, but under some circumstances may decide not to act empathically and *not* to act cooperatively in seeking a solution. Such a person may be said to lack a 'moral compass.' What can teachers do to help students to acquire the requisite values?

One approach is to provide students with a list of appropriate values[8] that are promoted by teachers and discussed with students. With younger students this approach can be effective, especially if the teacher is seen as having moral authority. With older students, who are typically more critical of teacher authority, a more indirect approach is better.

Positive values can be inculcated more surely if they are examined in the context of a practical issue that students are concerned about; for example, how they might react as bystanders witnessing a case of bullying.

This is my suggestion. Introduce a scenario in which students are observing bullying taking place, say in the school playground. After a brief discussion, ask students to record what they think *they* would do under such circumstances; would they, for instance, help the victim, inform a teacher or ignore the matter? Next ask them to provide brief explanations of why they would, or would not, undertake such actions.[9] Then read through the explanations, share them with the students (many will 'own' and justify them), and discuss the values that are implicit in what they have said. Many students will have made strong statements about the rightness of helping others when they are being bullied. There will be some who are unsure what they would do and are relatively lukewarm about taking any action. But invariably there will be many statements that reveal highly moral attitudes. What is fair, good, caring, thoughtful, considerate, compassionate, kind, brave, public-spirited – these and other such values come directly from what the students think and feel about a concrete situation, not from moralising pronouncements about what they ought to feel. Naturally enough they carry far more weight.[10]

The benefits of this activity are twofold. It can result in bullying being discouraged by students who have become motivated to intervene. This means that there may be fewer cases to deal with. Equally important is the effect it can have on the ethical judgements of students who participate in meetings in which the Method of Shared Concern is implemented.

Students as active collaborators

As we have seen, many students are not prepared to collaborate with teachers in addressing cases of bullying. They are commonly averse to informing on bullies. They don't think that teachers are either willing or able to help. As a consequence, many cases of bullying go unrecorded. As Pikas has put it, 'bullying goes on behind the backs of the teachers'. Students generally know who is being bullied. Teachers often do not. The question then is: how can students become motivated to seek the expert assistance of teachers for those in need?

This is a crucial problem for many schools, particularly secondary schools. Clearly it requires that teachers develop a relationship with their students such that the students see it as being in their interest to work with teachers in addressing bullying. Teachers need to be seen as credible practitioners of an intervention method; a method, moreover, that students are comfortable with. Generally speaking, students are not comfortable with a method that seeks – often unsuccessfully – to stop the bullying using a traditional punitive approach. Arguably, they can be persuaded to become collaborators if the method is genuinely non-punitive and they are treated with respect – whatever their history – and become partners in seeking an agreed outcome.

Working with subgroups of students at risk

Earlier it was suggested that a universal approach is desirable in educating students about bullying. A school may nevertheless decide that it would like to work more intensively with subgroups of students. These may consist of students who have been identified as needing special attention because of their frequent involvement in bully/victim problems as bullies, victims or bully–victims.

First, there are the students who are repeatedly being targeted by other, more dominating students and appear unable to protect themselves. There is much to be said for identifying such students early. As we know, they are at much greater risk than others of developing serious long-term mental problems such as severe social anxiety and depression. They need support. But in addition they can often be helped to acquire skills to become more assertive and better able to make friends – thereby reducing the chances of being victimised by peers.[11] Positive social skills – and the confidence their possession produces – can be very useful for repeated targets of bullying. And they can be most useful for targeted students if and when they find themselves engaged in negotiating with suspected bullies during the final stage of the application of the Method of Shared Concern,

Helping students whose behaviour suggests that they are likely to bully others is problematic. Unlike potential victims, they are generally not motivated to acquire attitudes and skills that can make life easier for themselves. They are often, in their own eyes, doing fine. Bringing together a group of students who are 'at risk' of bullying others – that is, aggressive and relatively insensitive children – and teaching them 'social skills' is frequently both difficult and unprofitable. As some researchers have shown, bullies often have in some respects above-average social intelligence.[12] They commonly have the social skills and simply prefer not to use them. I am aware of no studies in which bringing suspected bullies together in a group to teach them positive social values and appropriate ways of behaving has been successful, although I have noted that it is quite often attempted. Notice that in the Method of Shared Concern suspected bullies are brought together only after they have been worked with as individuals. Moreover, their presence in a group is to address a *specified case* of bullying in which they are involved. They are not simply students who have been identified as badly behaved and bullying other students. They are not being brought together to be 'straightened out'.

Nevertheless, individuals who commonly engage in bullying others can be helped to behave more constructively if they become involved in some way in a group whose behaviour is notably pro-social. Bear in mind that how an individual student behaves, even one who is predisposed to act aggressively, is determined to a large extent by the nature of the group pressure from the peers with whom he or she continually interacts. By arranging for aggressive or anti-social individuals to work and interact with a pro-social group, radical change in the motivation of those who are inclined to bully is always possible. This was confirmed for me several years ago at a secondary school in New South Wales where a school counsellor introduced the Method of Shared Concern. To help her with her work, she brought together a number of volunteers (two per class) to form a supportive anti-bullying committee. They helped in many ways, including bringing cases of bullying to the counsellor's attention. A dispute arose at one point over whether a particular student who had – quite unexpectedly – volunteered to be part of the anti-bullying committee should be admitted as a committee member. He had a reputation as a major bully. After much argumentation – and uncertainty – he was accepted as a member. In this new context his efforts to help counter bullying were outstanding. He strongly identified with the group and was in fact accepted as a leader. Subsequently he became a spokesperson for the group promoting the anti-bullying work of the school through numerous media engagements. Of course, this success story may not always be replicated. The anti-bullying committee took a risk. But it does illustrate the potential power of a new group environment in transforming behaviour.

Helping roles for groups of students

Utilising a subgroup of students trained to fulfil a special role in addressing problems of bullying has been a prominent feature of the anti-bullying work undertaken in many schools. Often the process is described as providing peer support or peer mediation or peer counselling.[13] Schools that employ this approach typically argue that:

- students generally have a better understanding of the problems experienced by their peers
- often teachers do not know what is going on – but students do
- students are generally more prepared to receive help from fellow students than from teachers
- some students are particularly apt at helping other students who are having difficulties with their peers
- these helpful students can be identified by the school and given appropriate training so that they can be more effective.

At the same time, some argue that even with exemplary training the selected students do not have sufficient authority to deal with intractable and serious problems of bullying; further, that creating an 'elite' of helpers is undesirable – for instance, it may place these students at some risk. Their peers may take exception to being spied on and informed about, as they see it, and decide to bully them.

My view is that, despite the risks and limitations that apply in promoting peer support activities undertaken by a subgroup of selected students, such activities can be helpful in bringing about a positive school ethos in which the Method of Shared Concern can be more effective. However, substantial effort must be made by the school in providing adequate training and monitoring. This is sometimes not provided, which may account for some peer support schemes being ineffective or even counterproductive. I think that if such schemes are to be optimally supportive of the Method of Shared Concern, the students being trained for the job should be fully instructed in how the method works. They can become ambassadors for the method; but only if they really understand it.

Can students apply the Method of Shared Concern?

It has been suggested by a correspondent at a school where the Method of Shared Concern is being implemented by trained staff members that the method could be taught to senior students and actually implemented by them. This is an interesting idea that is worth exploring. Certainly some secondary students are able to acquire the knowledge and skills to apply the method.

They are also likely to be more influential in some ways than teachers. Being closer psychologically to the students with whom they might work, their understanding and insights into student conflicts may put them at an advantage. Students with problems are more likely to approach them and be listened to.

At the same time, there are some limitations on what can be expected of senior students as appliers of the method. Most obviously, as we have seen, it can be time-consuming, both in acquiring adequate training and in applying it to particular cases. As well, from time to time cases will arise that in the judgement of a staff member require a disciplinary approach, which a student cannot reasonably be asked to handle.

There is a further reason why it is preferable for school staff to apply the method. The successful use of the method helps to build a bridge between the staff of a school and its students. This is especially important for students who have hitherto been distrustful of the school establishment. Many bullies fit into this category. When a school authority figure interacts with a student in a non-authoritarian manner a significant and positive change can take place in the student's way of thinking about relationships that up to then had been determined largely by the norms of the peer group.

My view therefore is that while the idea of students applying the method is in some ways attractive, it is much better for trained staff to be the practitioners. Nevertheless, as suggested earlier, students who have learned about the method can be more influential in interacting with the peers they seek to help. The technique of sharing concern about the victim with the bully is often a wiser and more effective way of helping the target than picking a fight over it. I conclude that it is inappropriate for students to become practitioners of the Method of Shared Concern – that is, to become solely responsible for dealing with a case of bullying. However, students who do come to understand the philosophy and rationale of the method may influence those who are in conflict without placing themselves personally at risk.

Parents

Because the Method of Shared Concern is not concerned with extreme or criminal forms of bullying, this method is generally seen as consistent with the work undertaken by schools *in loco parentis*. This imposing Latin phrase does not, however, provide clear indications of what a school can or cannot do in its role 'in the place of a parent.' Local and community factors are likely to influence how the principle is understood, and some fluidity or flexibility is to be expected in its interpretation. It is fair to say that many parents feel they should become involved if their child is being bullied; the same is true, to a lesser extent, of the parents of the suspected bully. On the other hand, exponents of the Method of Shared Concern (following Pikas) argue that many cases of bullying are best handled without any parental involvement. How can potential conflicts between teachers and parents on this matter best be handled?

Part of the answer may lie in clarifying what is meant by 'bullying'. If it is regarded, as it is by some bullying 'experts', as a crime, then parents should always be involved. However, the law does not recognise bullying *per se* as a legal offence, although some forms of bullying are criminal and therefore can be categorised as punishable offences. The trouble is that we have one word, bullying, to describe a range of qualitatively different behaviours – from mild verbal taunting to vicious physical assaults. The first task in making a case for the use of the Method of Shared Concern without parental involvement is to differentiate between degrees of severity of bullying, and to convince parents that it is reasonable to identify an area of bullying behaviour that schools can handle *in loco parentis*; that is, as parents would normally handle such a case in their own families. This is no easy matter, as parents are likely to have different opinions about where to draw the line.

Apart from questions of definition and legal responsibility, there looms the question in the minds of some parents of whether the Method of Shared Concern is an appropriate method of intervention and, if so, for what kinds of cases. If the method is to be introduced, the school has a responsibility to explain to parents what it is about. Many parents will not have heard about it. Some will have inaccurate or distorted views on what it is. It follows that the school must explain what is involved.

These points can reasonably be made in explaining the Method of Shared Concern to parents:

- **The school is committed to taking whatever action is deemed necessary to ensure the safety of all students.** The Method of Shared Concern is *one* of a range of methods being used to by the school to counter bullying
- **The method is not applicable to criminal forms of bullying.** For such behaviour disciplinary methods are regarded as more appropriate.
- **Although practitioners of the method do not accuse any students of engaging in bullying, it requires that those who have been involved, whether as perpetrators, victims or bystanders, to accept responsibility,** individually and collectively, in helping to fix the problem.
- **The safety of the victim can more readily be achieved through adopting a non-punitive approach,** and empowering those involved to negotiate an ending to the bullying.
- **There is strong evidence that the Method of Shared Concern can achieve a very high level of success** when employed by a trained practitioner in appropriate cases.
- **The Method of Shared Concern is an approach supported by research** conducted on behalf of the Australian Federal Government through the Department of Employment, Education and Workplace Relations (DEEWR).[14]

When it is introduced, an outline of the method with appropriate references should be provided to the parents of students attending the school. Meetings may also be arranged for interested parents to discuss the method.

Although a carefully presented case for the use of the method can be expected to result generally in parental cooperation, this is not always the case, especially on the part of parents who are incensed by the harm that has been done to their child and who demand that the perpetrator be punished. This is understandable, and it needs to be handled patiently. Make it clear that the bullies are not being let off. They are in fact being held responsible for helping to fix the problem. Bear in mind that the primary concern of parents is the safety of their child at school. They may come to see that the use of punishment directed towards the perpetrator can often further endanger the person who has been targeted; and that both goals – the punishment of the offender and the safety of the offended – are difficult to ensure, as the bullying can and often does continue in subtle and covert ways that are no less distressing to the victim. When this is explained to parents the method is almost always accepted.

Leadership

Leadership is a much touted concept. It conjures up in some people Napoleon exhorting his men into battle, or Shakespeare's Henry V declaiming 'once more into the breach, dear friends!' Spectacular claims of what can be achieved may be misplaced, unrealistic and produce a cynical response, as in this piece of dialogue from Shakespeare's *Henry IV Part 1*:

> ***Glendower***: *I can call spirits from the vasty deep.*
>
> ***Hotspur***: *Why so can I, and so can any man. But will they come when you do call for them?*

Effective leadership in this, as in many areas, is far more likely to be achieved through careful planning than by charisma. Part of that preparation must be the acquisition of a sound knowledge of the Method of Shared Concern on the part of the principal and others who can provide the necessary leadership. Surprisingly, I have known schools in which the principal is aware that the method is being used at his school without any comprehension of its nature and rationale, and how it can be distinguished from other forms of intervention. It is not essential that principals be trained in the use of Method of Shared Concern (though some are) or have direct experience in its application. But they must at least be able to identify its major features, explain its rationale, and say why it may be used on occasions in preference or in addition to other approaches in dealing with cases of bullying.

The tasks facing the principal in introducing and justifying the use of the Method of Shared Concern may be described as follows.

1. **The principal should ensure that there is acceptance of the method by the staff as a viable approach to handling cases of bullying.** Clearly the staff must be well informed, and have participated in appraising the value and practicality of its use. Any reservations on the part of individual staff

members should be addressed: opposition should never be steamrollered. Especially, it is necessary to specify and discuss the situations or circumstances in which the method may – or may not – be used. Evidence for its effectiveness must be weighed against the costs to the school in time spent implementing the procedures and the training that is needed.

2. **Individual staff members who will be most affected by the implementation of the method should be identified.** They will normally include the school counsellor and staff who have undertaken responsibilities in behaviour management. It should be acknowledged that at times these people may have contrasting roles in the school, with the former being concerned primarily with non-punitive means of influencing students and the latter with taking disciplinary action. Achieving a collaborative relationship between staff with potentially conflicting roles is an extremely important task for the principal. It requires a clear understanding of the circumstances under which the Method of Shared Concern can legitimately be employed, and when disciplinary action may be preferable. Principles and procedures must be devised to reach such decisions.
3. **Effective staff training must be arranged.** Without this, introducing the Method of Shared Concern is unlikely to achieve the best outcomes for the school. Hence the need to acquire resources, including relevant literature, DVDs and (most importantly) individuals experienced in the use of the method who can provide appropriate instruction (see Appendix 6).
4. **The support of parents must be obtained.** While gaining support for the Method of Shared Concern within the school is a necessary starting point, there remains the task of ensuring that parents are also supportive. This can be a challenge (see above) that should not be underestimated, given a tendency in some communities to believe that a traditional disciplinary approach is required in *all* cases of bullying.
5. **It should not be assumed that leadership in this area is entirely the province of the school principal.** He or she must carry the main responsibility for the enterprise, but in any school there will be individuals who because of their roles or their personal interest in the method can be highly influential. Obviously these will include those who undertake to apply the method. Their effectiveness and the example they set will be a

major factor in the success or otherwise of the venture. In addition, there may be students or groups of students who see in the use of the method a means by which conflicts between students can be resolved for the good of everybody – and seek to influence other students so that they will cooperate more fully and effectively with teachers in handling cases of bullying. Their support is crucial. In the end it will be largely through their efforts that the Method of Shared Concern can ultimately be successful.

The potential contribution of the Method of Shared Concern to world peace

A primary concern of schools must be the wellbeing of students during their time at school. The appeal of the Method of Shared Concern lies first in its capacity to involve students in solving problems of interpersonal conflict at school. But its relevance to social education extends much further. When students learn to deal constructively with interpersonal conflict at school, it might reasonably be expected that they will apply the acquired skills in dealing with problems that arise in future contexts such as those occurring in the workplace and the home. We could also bring about a new generation of people who may make much more positive contributions to world peace.

Nations at times employ bullying tactics to impose themselves on other nations. Indeed, a great deal of recorded history is about such impositions – and the wars that have followed. There is a parallel between the behaviour of those who make decisions on behalf of nations to threaten and attack others and the behaviour of bullies in the school yard.[15] And, it may be added, the parallel extends to the behaviour of those who passively observe: the bystanders. In recent years, the urgency of applying problem-solving skills to preserve international peace has become much more acute as the possibility of nuclear annihilation for all parties becomes more real.

Pikas is one who believes that the effective training of schoolchildren in the means by which they can reach shared conclusions about how to resolve conflict is vital at this stage in history. He writes[16]:

> In the student turmoil year of 1968, the concept of peace education was created. I participated in international conferences for this new approach. Being a Professor in educational psychology at Uppsala University, it was natural for me to maintain that peace ideals should be operationalised in exercises of conflict resolution in schools. As parties in international conflicts start wars claiming their being a victim and blaming the antagonist being a bully, I focused my field applications on asymmetric conflicts amongst teenagers, called group bullying.

My experiments were successful; I became Visiting Professor of Peace Education in the U.S., Canada and West Germany. Teenagers liked my Shared Concern method (SCm) because of the voluntary ingredient in it. After discussing with teenagers 'How to deal with bullying' they gave me the names of 'classmates who need help'. These were immediately treated. Teenagers became interested in applying therapeutic mediation in their conflicts. So I developed, within a device, called All in the Class Become Mediators, ACBM, role plays. Teachers found to fit well to their vernacular language training syllabus. (Instruction is at my home-site http://www.pikas.se/scm/) A trustful atmosphere is thereby created with socially deviant students. Investigations are planned to obtain evidence about preventive effects against any future criminal behaviour.

SCm is derived from the great shared concern paradigm that is growing in collective consciousness in our world. Awareness is rising: global climate deterioration depends on increasing and consuming world population. Humankind is at a crossroad: either to implement a shared solution paradigm or face the fact that the most effective means for diminishing the population stress – the nuclear holocaust – will, sooner or later, be released in some international conflict.

The paradigm of shared concern has implications also for the resolution of ethnic conflicts around the world. In 2003 I was invited to give workshops in Estonia; I have repeated these by yearly visits, and SCm became used more extensively. In 2010 ethnic Russians, about one third of the Estonian population, joined SCm courses. So far, it is just implied that SCm, used in resolving school conflicts including bullying, will make a prototype for solving ethnic tensions between Estonians and Russians.[17] If it happens that politicians and principals realise that our public school systems can become an instrument for a global conflict management education, they hopefully realise that this education has to go beyond repeating well-meant declarations. It has to be based on learning-by-doing devices, reinforced by treatment of actual cases of asymmetric conflicts, called bullying.

Those teenagers who get the point with the above peace education will, within 5–10 years, become voters and political leaders. As soon as the leaders of nations and schools realise what skills of reaching shared solutions can achieve for their own nation or their own school, a global movement of implementing will start.

The wider community as well as the narrower school environment can benefit enormously from the mediational skills that can be developed among students. This realisation can act as a powerful motivator for the introduction of the method.

Endnotes

1. In a study of 14-year-old Australian students some 40 per cent reported that teachers were not really interested in taking action to stop bullying. Among those identified as 'victims', the percentage was higher. (Rigby & Bagshaw, 2003).
2. Many of these suggestions are currently being implemented by MindMatters, an Australian government-funded organisation providing a professional development program for secondary schools. It is concerned with promoting the wellbeing and safety of school students largely through the school curriculum, and contains a wide range of activities and resources designed to help teachers work with students on issues relating to bullying. See <http://www.mindmatters.edu.au/default.asp>.
3. See Bellhouse (2009) for practical instruction on the use of circle time.
4. Pluralistic ignorance involves a failure to appreciate the fact that other people are as concerned and sensitive as you are about how others feel (see Allport, 1924).
5. Cooperative learning is a process that enables students to work with their peers to accomplish a shared or common goal. The goal is reached through group members working interdependently rather than alone. For an account of how it was introduced and evaluated in a school, see Cowie et al. (1994).
6. The tendency for both bullies and victims to be more averse than other students to taking part in cooperative activities was reported by Rigby, Cox and Black (1997).
7. In a study conducted by McLoughlin (2009) with 12-year-old schoolchildren in Ohio the Positive Peer Group Program was shown to produce significant improvements in positive attitudes and behaviours; for instance, in problem-solving and behavioural accountability.
8. In Australia the federal government has endorsed the following as key values to be taught to students: care and compassion; doing your best; a fair go; freedom; honesty and trustworthiness; integrity; respect; responsibility; understanding, tolerance and inclusion. See <http://www.curriculum.edu.au/verve/_resources/Framework_PDF_version_for_the_web.pdf>.
9. See Blake, Rigby and Johnson (2004) for an account of how this approach was employed in an Australian primary school.
10. The influence of adults, both teachers and parents, has been shown to be much weaker than that of fellow students in determining how students are prepared to act as bystanders witnessing bullying behaviour among their peers. See Rigby and Johnson (2006).
11. How teachers and counsellors can assist vulnerable students in effectively resisting those who would bully them is discussed at length in chapter 4, 'Strengthening the victim', in Rigby (2010b).
12. This finding, surprising to some, was reported by Kaukiainen et al. (1999) among students attending schools in Finland. It applied especially to students who engaged in more indirect forms of bullying.
13. For a thoughtful examination of peer mediation in schools see Cremin (2007).
14. See Rigby and Griffiths (2010).
15. A discussion of the implications of bullying in schools for aggression between nations can be found in Rigby (2006).
16. From a letter received from Pikas, cited with his permission.
17. Courses on SCm are being provided by the Estonian Union of Child Welfare. Contact merit@lastekaitseliit.ee<mailto:merit@lastekaitseliit.ee>.

Chapter 7 Professional development and the Method of Shared Concern

This final chapter explains how I think education about the Method of Shared Concern can be included in the professional development of teachers and counsellors. Ideally it should be undertaken in pre-service courses in schools of education in teacher training centres. With some notable exceptions, education about bullying in schools and what to do about it is largely neglected in pre-service courses[1]; teaching about the Method of Shared Concern even more so. It is generally left to educational consultants to provide instruction and guidance through in-service sessions. In an increasing number of schools it fits well within what schools provide through professional development.

Books are all very well – for some people. But for some they do not engage or motivate, at least not as much as actively working with others in pursuit of a common goal. In any case, it really is far from easy to get an overburdened school staff, or even most of them, to find time to read a book, including this one, as a means of exploring the Method of Shared Concern. (I am banking on at least one bibliophile in a school being an exception!) But even if I am wrong – as I hope I am – there is a great deal more that can be gained by interested staff members meeting together, discussing ideas and sharing experiences and trying new things out. In short, there is a lot more that can be done, especially in what has come to be called workshopping.

Suppose a school wants to workshop the Method of Shared Concern: how can it go about it? Well, there is no simple answer. We have to begin by asking a few questions.

The most important question is: Why should a school want to do it? A frequent answer goes something like this. Somebody has been to an anti-bullying conference or has read a book or on article or heard a talk on the radio or seen somebody talking on TV or heard from a friend or from a teacher at another school ... and it seems like a good idea. Further, it is known that the minister of education and the department are supportive.[2] Curiosity has been aroused. True, a few cynics are shaking their heads; a few are muttering about crackpot radicals or yet another fast-fading fad. However, there is sufficient interest, and it is decided to give it a go and invite a suitable expert along.

The visiting guru duly appears – and with no more ado begins a series of role plays (just what kind, we will come to). In no time the room is abuzz with counsellors, bullies and victims, interacting like mad, sharing their concerns. Time goes quickly. Hardly time to complete all of what was intended, or to debrief. The attendees troop out. What was that all about, they say.

This is a not altogether inaccurate description of what can and sometimes does happen when interest has been aroused, but there has been insufficient consideration of the needs, perceptions and motivations of a school staff. In the school I have just imagined there is no preliminary examination of what is involved in adopting the Method of Shared Concern. Probably no-one has seen it work. There are massive misconceptions about it. Some are vaguely prejudiced against it, some equally vaguely for it. There is certainly a good deal of curiosity, but no more than a few committed in any way to acquiring the necessary knowledge and skills to practise the method. At this point there is little point in plunging straight into a series of role plays on how you do it. There must be some reasonable sort of preparation.

For many schools I believe the starting point is first addressing bullying *in general*, then the Method of Shared Concern. Begin with a definition of bullying, the forms it takes, the harm it does, and (what is not often recognised) a recognition that progress in reducing bullying is being gradually made, despite the many, many failures incurred in addressing this very difficult problem. This may be followed by an outline of what schools are actually doing proactively and reactively – yes, reactively – we are not reacting well enough. Bullying just keeps on happening, at times, apparently staunchlessly. We need to get our heads around the way we are reacting to cases of bullying, or – if 'reacting' has become too imbued with political incorrectness – what actions we are taking that only work sometimes (if at all), and in some circumstances (but not others). It is often sensible to keep the role plays in reserve, or use them sparingly, until there is a consensus on what the staff thinks needs to be done.

Now consider another school. Here there has already been a preliminary discussion of school bullying, followed by a thoughtful examination of a range of interventional approaches. Discussion has centred not on what is *best*, but rather on what are the pros and cons of each approach, and when each might be the most appropriate . Steps have already been taken to examine the Method of Shared Concern by some staff members. It has already been tried out, more or less experimentally. It seems to have been successful. However, there are lots of questions that need to be asked. In what sort of cases can it be applied? Many of the questions are of the 'what if' variety. What if the suspected bullies don't cooperate? What if they lie? What if it is felt that no group meetings are needed? What if there is nobody properly trained to do it? What if the target is unwilling to come to a meeting with the suspected bullies? What if it takes too long? What if parents object? What if the bullying starts up again? What if a crime has been committed? Questions like these need to be raised or foreshadowed as soon as an outline of the method has been grasped. The answers will become clearer as the method is explored in greater depth.

In the case of the relatively well prepared school we must next try to develop a deeper understanding not only of the rationale of the method but also just what happens when a practitioner undertakes to use this approach. Here role plays become essential.

Planning a workshop

Anybody who has tried to plan a workshop will know that there are at least three important considerations that affect what can be done. These are:

- the **time** that is being made available
- the **place** where the workshop is to be held

- the **resources** available to the presenter.

Each can play a determining role in what is done, and in how it is done.

Time

Time is often at a premium in schools. Different topics and activities compete for the time that could be available for professional development. Bullying gets much greater consideration when there has been a major problem at a school, for example when a child has been seriously assaulted, a parent has decided to sue and the media are on to it. The danger here is that the school may be under pressure to endorse tough, draconian – and generally popular – practices in addressing cases. A dispassionate examination of alternatives, especially non-punitive ones, may be difficult. A cynic might observe that the school's response to a crisis is political rather than one likely to lead to more enlightened practices. Ideally, adequate time is allotted regardless of the current – and possibly exceptional – situation.

But what is 'adequate'? Here, of course, it is necessary to consult the declared aims for the meeting. As suggested these may vary widely, from providing a general overview of current thinking about bullying and methods of intervention, including the Method of Shared Concern, to a more in-depth examination of the rationale and detailed application of the method. The latter will be more time-consuming.

A one-hour meeting may sometimes be enough for providing basic information on the Method of Shared Concern, especially for people to whom the method is new. Such a meeting could include:

- **a brief introduction to bullying in schools** and how schools are responding to the problem
- **a description of the Method of Shared Concern** and its rationale
- **an examination of the method's claims** as an appropriate and effective way of dealing with some cases of bullying.

From discussion after the presentation it should be possible to gauge whether the school staff is ready to adopt the method (among others) and receive further training in its use. It may be possible after such a meeting to identify individuals who are interested in receiving more specialist training and take a lead in applying the method.

At *this* stage planning a longer period of time for such a meeting *with everybody* may not be a good idea. Some staff members may reasonably think that the approach could be useful but do not feel that they personally want to apply it. Yet others may be curious and want to learn more before they commit themselves to applying it. A list of resources should be made available (see appendix 6), together with copies of selected papers. These can help staff members to think it over.

When more time is available for personal development on the method, *and* there is a group of staff who already have some background in the method and its use, a more ambitious workshop can be devised. Examples of how such workshops may be conducted will be described presently. To state the obvious: morning is the best time to hold a workshop. The worst time is late afternoon, especially if the meeting pushes on over the time teachers are normally packing up and going home. Then the meeting seems to the members like an imposition.

Place

It is sometimes not realised that the success or failure of professional development sessions can depend on the place where the meeting is held. Some meetings cannot be run effectively unless the place is right. This is certainly true for the Method of Shared Concern, especially when use is made of role plays and related exercises.

I have learned this the hard way, turning up at a school with a careful and detailed plan for a half-day workshop only to discover that it was to be held in a scarcely possible environment. These were its features:

- rows of immovable seats sloping upwards from the front
- over 80 closely packed staff members, so that it was only possible to speak personally with those at the edges during any activities – people in the middle were not accessible
- terrible acoustics, with noises in the room continually amplified
- poor lighting, making it hard for some to read the handouts
- delays of some 15 minutes before the PowerPoints worked, sadly not unusual.

I learned that if it is at all possible the presenter should know about the place *before* the workshop is held. Ideally this means visiting the place and examining its potential – and perhaps advising on its suitability – well before the workshop is to be held. This is rarely done. As a result, the presenter often has to modify or even abandon what has been planned and improvise on the spot.

What sort of space, furnishings and conditions are usually needed for running a workshop on the Method of Shared Concern? Here is my wish list:

- **Plenty of space.** This is important, especially if you want to run a series of exercises with multiple subgroups of people interacting simultaneously. For instance, you may want to conduct role plays with teams of people in twos and threes or fours. The small groupings need to be far enough apart not to distract one another
- **No rows of seats, no fixed chairs.** Chairs that can easily be moved around, light ones
- **No tables.** Having tables with half a dozen or more sitting at each is quite common and well intentioned. So too are the strategically placed lollies. But conversation at the tables is often not easy for people at the extremities. If you want to have counselling-type interactions or simulations of small group meetings (as I do) then such tables are irrelevant, and they take up a lot of room
- **Everyone, presenter and others, at the same level**, no raised platforms, no slopes upwards or downwards
- **A room off the main room** where the presenter can talk with a subgroup of members briefly away from the rest, privately, if need be (sometimes it is useful to give subgroups different instructions)
- **A truly reliable IT person** at hand, if DVDs or PowerPoints are being used
- **An assistant** who will nimbly distribute handouts
- **A comfortable temperature**, not too warm.

Resources

What resources are most useful for educating or training in the Method of Shared Concern? In part, it will depend on what stage has been reached in its consideration of the method. Once the method has been adopted, more specialised resources are required (see Appendix 6); some may be developed by the school to explain what it has decided to do. Different versions may be needed for staff members and for parents.

Resources on the Method of Shared Concern may be divided into published books and papers; PowerPoints; and audio-visual resources.

Published books and papers

These are listed in appendix 6. Some of these provide an introduction to the method; others offer a more in-depth examination of its application, rationale and effectiveness.

PowerPoints

PowerPoint presentations can be very useful mainly in providing factual content, and can be developed to structure presentations. However, it is worth noting the spreading disillusion about their indiscriminate use. Recently I was told that I could present at a conference in Germany on the understanding that I did not bring any PowerPoint slides! The perceived need, common among presenters, to stick very closely to the content of every slide, even when it is redundant, and to lose touch with an audience who want *their* issues addressed, can lead to a loss of interest.

Audiovisual resources

Audiovisual resources may be very useful in helping a school staff to understand and evaluate the Method of Shared Concern. They may include the following.

- **A staff training DVD**, made by Readymade Productions in 2007, shows how the method can be applied, and describes the method using a series of role plays involving practitioners and students.[3] The first shows how the method can be used with boys, the second with girls. The process is essentially the same for either sex, but, as one might expect, the girls are more willing and perhaps more able to verbalise their feelings and engage in discussion about the situation with the practitioner. The DVD is accompanied by a booklet that provides further explanations to complement the film. For single-sex schools it is suggested that either the first part (involving boys) or the second part (involving girls) is used. The DVD takes 50 minutes to view. A ninety-minute to two-hour period is needed to include introduction and discussion time. It is most important that the DVD is both introduced *and* discussed afterwards. I have known viewers to be very puzzled or frustrated when the DVD has not been placed in context. The booklet to the DVD suggests discussion questions.

A word of warning about the DVD. Although it conveys the procedure well and illustrates the non-punitive and supportive roles employed by the practitioners, the outcomes were ones that the students decided upon themselves. In the case of the boys this was a resolution to stop bullying the target, but *without* any genuine negotiation or expressed regard for him. One shortcoming in the DVD was the failure to engage the students in a serious discussion in the penultimate group meeting in *devising a plan* on how they would negotiate a resolution of the problem with the target. Attention should be drawn to the importance of doing this.

- **The DVD *Bullying in schools: six basic methods of intervention,*** produced by Loggerheads, can be used especially in helping staff to see the Method of Shared Concern in the context of five other methods of intervention.[4] It does not explicitly promote the method; rather it provides examples of how different methods may be used, and enables viewers to form a judgement about their comparative advantages and possible limitations. I should add that in this DVD a relatively large number of students are included in illustrating the method. Normally the number of students involved in the Method of Shared Concern is small, being around three or four.
- **Vodcasts** on bullying in schools developed by the Queensland Department of Education and Training may be viewed online.[5] These are supplemented by a number of articles and other resources that can be downloaded. The set of six vodcasts may be viewed as a comprehensive account of how bullying can be addressed by schools. Vodcasts 4 and 5 deal with intervention methods, and include an examination of the Method of Shared Concern.

Role plays

Training in the Method of Shared Concern can be greatly facilitated through the use of role plays. Role plays may be carried out:

- by members in front of the whole group, or
- in small groups, each with a member acting as observer.

Role plays in front of the whole group may be performed by:

1. **individuals who have been instructed and prepared beforehand** by the workshop presenter to demonstrate the method. These may include the presenter and people with whom the presenter has previously worked
2. **members of the group** who have been learning about the method during the workshop and who volunteer to role play what they have learnt
3. **members of the group who are each required** to demonstrate in turn how they would perform a given role. This is the method preferred by Pikas, who also video-records each performance for a subsequent examination by the group. This method is time-consuming, and is threatening to some members who opt out.

Role plays *not* in front of the group may be performed simultaneously by members in small groups in different parts of the workshop, following detailed instructions. This is much less threatening to participants. However, it is important to ensure that each role play is well conducted and that feedback is received by other group members. To achieve this, a person is nominated to act as an observer during each of the role plays and report back to the entire workshop afterwards.

How many role plays there will be, and what kind, will be determined by the aims of the meeting, the time available, the place where the meeting is held and the numbers of participants. Numbers clearly matter a good deal, as does the motivation of participants. Generally I have found that groups of over 30 are difficult to handle if role plays other than those performed in front of the group are used. An ideal number is around 15.

Role plays *may* be conducted simultaneously in small groups even with relatively large numbers if members are very well motivated; if, for example, they are teachers and counsellors who have chosen to come to the workshop and are keen to practise the method. It should nevertheless be borne in mind that the larger the group, the less attention can be paid to each participant.

Using the role plays

Here are some suggestions as to how role plays may be used. Detailed instructions are given in appendix 2. It is important that these are clearly understood before the role plays begin. Participants should not discuss the instructions for their particular role with one another before commencement.

If there is only time for one role play, use role play 1. Afterwards the workshop presenter will need to explain and discuss what happens next.

1. **The practitioner and a suspected bully** Members work in threes: one takes the role of the practitioner, another the suspected bully, the third an observer. This role play may take five to 10 minutes. The observer may take notes, but not the practitioner. Feedback from each role play can subsequently be provided by the observer to the entire workshop.
2. **The practitioner and a series of suspected bullies seen in turn** Members work in fives. In addition to the practitioner and observer, there are three suspected bullies, each with different clearly described characteristics. Each suspected bully is interviewed in turn. Those waiting to be interviewed must be out of earshot. After each suspected bully has been interviewed he or she may join the observer, but importantly may not act in any way to influence the interactions with the practitioner. Observers report back to the entire workshop.
3. **The practitioner and the targeted student** Members work in threes: the practitioner, the target and an observer. It is suggested that the target for this role play be a person who has been an observer previously. Again the observers report back and issues are explored.

Once role plays 2 and 3 have been completed, the next two role plays may be undertaken by a team of players who are prepared to perform *in front of the other workshop members.*

4. **The practitioner and a group of suspected bullies** In this role play, members who have already played the part of suspected bullies in an earlier role play are involved, together with the person who acted as the practitioner.
5. **The summit meeting: the practitioner and a group of suspected bullies plus the target** This meeting begins without the target being present, to

briefly prepare the group for what is to follow. When the practitioner and the group are ready, they are joined by the person who played the target in a previous role play with the practitioner.

Depending on how many role plays the workshop presenter decides to have performed, more than one session may be needed. Role plays 4 and 5 can best be performed *after a break* between sessions during which those who have agreed to take part are briefed. The aim in the final role play is to illustrate how a positive solution can be attained.

Assessment

The desirability of feedback from workshop members is now unquestioned, but the nature of the questions worth asking can be controversial. Rather than ask members how pleased or otherwise they were with what happened, I think it is better to seek information first about what was learned. Some of what may have been learned can be assessed through a knowledge test of the Method of Shared Concern (there is one in appendix 5). Useful though this test may be, it does not test whether the learner has acquired *relevant skills*, or an appreciation of what skills are worth developing.

Skills can, of course, be best appraised by observers. To some extent appraisal may come through feedback provided at a workshop. But it must be recognised that what a trainee practitioner does at a workshop under the gaze of critical peers may not be a good indicator of how he or she will perform in practice. As noted earlier, having an observer/appraiser present when the method is used *for real* at a school with students is considered unacceptable, as it is likely to affect the quality of the relationship that the practitioner is seeking to develop. Hence, self-rating of skills as they develop becomes a very important element in assessing competence. The practitioner needs to ask continually: Has the way I have interacted with this student and with this group brought us any nearer to a non-coercive, agreed solution to the problem? And what was it I did to enable this to happen, or fail to happen?

Finally there is one simple question that must be asked: Do the members believe that they would actually apply what they have learnt? My experience is that overwhelmingly they say they will.

Endnotes

1. The inadequacy of pre-service education has been demonstrated through surveys of teachers in training in both the United States and England. See Bauman and Del Rio (2005).
2. At least this is the case in Australia. Following the publication online of the report 'Applying the Method of Shared Concern in Australian schools: an evaluative study' (Rigby & Griffiths, 2010) the then minister for education. Julia Gillard, provided a media release commending its use by schools. See <http://www.deewr.gov.au/Ministers/Gillard/Media/Releases/Pages/Article_100118_085945.aspx>.
3. See Readymade Productions (2007).
4. See Rigby, K. (2009b). *Bullying in schools: six methods of intervention*. Loggerhead Productions.
5. Vodcasts developed for the Queensland Department of Education and Training describing a range of intervention methods, including the Method of Shared Concern (Rigby, 2009a), may be accessed at <http://education.qld.gov.au/studentservices/protection/community/bullying.html>.

Postscript

A little while ago an article appeared in an education journal in Australia on the Method of Shared Concern.[1] It was based upon what I had said in an interview, and was generally accurate and positive. I could find no fault with the text. However, down the right hand side of the first page of the article was a picture of a tall flagpole with a white flag fluttering in the breeze.

I asked the editor about it and learned that it was meant to symbolise peace. I have no reason to believe there was any other motive. Yet it continued to bother me. Perhaps it was because I am just old enough to remember the stirring speeches of Mr Churchill during the Second World War, and especially his famous words 'we shall never surrender.'

The suggestion seemed to be that in applying the Method of Shared Concern we were showing the white flag and surrendering to the bullies. I know that many people see it that way. They believe that the only way to beat the bullies is to declare war on them. Tackling the problem of bullying is a war between the good guys (like us) and the bad guys (like them).

Well, if we continue to see it that way the Method of Shared Concern will not stand a chance. The very act of sitting down with the enemy will be seen as a kind of treachery. If we meet with them at all, it will be to assert what we already know about them. We will refuse to listen. We will refuse to even countenance the possibility that these bad guys will ever recognise and acknowledge that someone has been and is being hurt and actually needs help. We will insist that *they* surrender; that *they* hoist the white flag, not us.

Fortunately it is now known that for the most part students who have taken part in bullying and are individually interviewed can be brought to see that someone they have bullied is distressed and, if they (the perpetrators) are treated with respect (a big 'if' in many bully/teacher encounters), they will agree to help, or fall in with a plan to help. And that which was virtually impossible to achieve in the first instance – the necessary cooperation of the whole group to which they belong in finding an acceptable solution to the problem – can ultimately be achieved. Only then can there be no victim; no bullies.

These prosaic facts are not known or believed by many of the critics of the Method of Shared Concern. So the task of stopping the bullying continues to be addressed as if it were a war – and the advocates of the method are seen as wavers of the white flag. Well, that must never be. The practitioners of Shared Concern are as committed as anyone that the bullies will not get their way and the targets will be made safe. They are the Churchillians who will never surrender. But they have their own way of gaining a victory.

Endnote

1. The article appeared in *Education Today*, Term 2, 2010, pp. 26–27, and was entitled 'Talking to stop bullying.'

Appendix 1 Case record of intervention using the Method of Shared Concern

1. Nature of the bullying as reported and sources of the information

   ____

   ____

2. Meetings with suspected bullies

   Dates: SB1 ______ SB2 ______ SB3 ______ SB4 ______ SB5 ______

	SB acknowledged some concern	SB promised to help	Action of SB later confirmed
SB1			
SB2			
SB3			
SB4			
SB5			

Comments: ____________________________________

____

____

3. Meeting with targeted student

   Date: ________

   T accepted help from practitioner: ________

   Role played by T as a *passive* victim or a *provocative* victim: ____________

   Comments: ____

   ____

   ____

4. Meeting with group of SBs

   Date: ________

   Proposed plan or proposal to which SBs agreed: ______________________

   ____

   ____

5. Summit meeting

   Date: ________

   Perceived outcome: (a) positive (b) uncertain (c) unsuccessful

   Comments: ____

   ____

   ____

6. Individual follow-up meetings with SBs

   Dates: SB1 _______ SB2 ________ SB3 ________ SB4 ________ SB5 ________

   Outcome (summarised): ______________________________________

   ____

   ____

7. Follow-up meeting with T

   Date: ________

   Outcome: (a) bullying stopped (b) bullying lessened (c) no change
   (d) bullying increased

   Comments: ____

   ____

   ____

8. Is any future action to be undertaken in relation to this case?

   ____

   ____

9. Conclusions and what has been learned from this application.

   ____

   ____

   ____

   ____

Appendix 2 The role plays

This appendix contains detailed instructions for the five role plays briefly described on pages 129–30. Select the ones you wish to use and *make copies for each of the players*. Ensure that each receives only the one that is relevant to his or her role.

10. The practitioner and a suspected bully
11. The practitioner and a series of suspected bullies seen in turn
12. The practitioner and the targeted student
13. The practitioner and a group of suspected bullies
14. The summit meeting – practitioner and a group of suspected bullies plus the target

For role plays that are not presented in front of workshop members, there must be an observer whose role is to report back to the others.

Role play 1: The practitioner and a suspected bully

Instructions for the practitioner

The student you are to meet is aged 14 years. You are a **teacher or counsellor** at the school. You have not met the student before.

You have learned **from others** that another student called Edward has been having a hard time. He has appeared upset and depressed. He has been staying away from school and unable to concentrate on schoolwork. You are hoping to learn more about why he is in such a state, and how he can be helped.

You have heard that Edward has been verbally abused and occasionally pushed around by members of the first student's friendship group. Rumours have been spread that he is gay. He has been receiving abusive text messages. He is very much on his own, and desperately miserable.

The student you are to meet is in the same class as Edward. He or she used to be in the same friendship group, and should be able to add to the picture and maybe help.

Follow this procedure:

1. **Greet** the student in a firm but friendly manner.
2. Explain briefly **who you are** and **why** you have asked him or her to talk with you; that is, because you are **concerned about Edward**.
3. **Share what you have heard or noticed about how Edward is feeling**; that he has appeared upset, lonely and quite depressed. Make no accusations. Make it clear that nobody is going to be in trouble about it.
4. Ask the student what he has noticed about Edward recently. (Your aim here is to **get some acknowledgement** that Edward is having a hard time.)
5. As soon as there is any recognition that things are not so good for Edward, ask: **What can we do about it?**
6. **Listen to suggestions** – or make some yourself. Reinforce any positive responses.
7. Explain that you will be **talking to other students** about how the situation can be improved.
8. End on a positive note, but **arrange for another meeting at a definite time** to see how things have progressed.

Instructions for the suspected bully

You are asked to play the role of a member of a group of students who have been involved in some way in bullying another student called Edward.

Edward used to be a friend, but recently your group have turned against him and have been giving him a hard time.

Edward has been verbally abused and occasionally pushed around by members of your friendship group. Rumours have been spread that he is gay. He has been receiving abusive text messages. As a result Edward is very much on his own, and desperately miserable.

There are times when you feel a bit sorry for Edward, but **when you are with your friends**, you realise that he probably deserves what he gets. After all, he has done some things that have made everyone in your group dislike him.

In fact you enjoy making fun of Edward, and you don't like the idea of going against the group.

One day a teacher you do not know comes into your class and asks to see you in private. You go along, without knowing what it is about.

Role play 2: The practitioner and a series of suspected bullies seen in turn

Instructions for the practitioner

There are three suspected bullies to be seen **in turn**: A, then B, then C. Again there will be an observer, who can take notes.

1. **Greet** the student in a firm but friendly manner.
2. Explain briefly **who you are** and **why** you have asked him or her to talk with you; that is, because you are **concerned about Edward**.
3. **Share what you have heard or noticed about how Edward is feeling**; that he has appeared upset, lonely and quite depressed. Make no accusations. Make it clear that nobody is going to be in trouble about it.
4. Ask the student what he has noticed about Edward recently. (Your aim here is to **get some acknowledgement** that Edward is having a hard time.)
5. As soon as there is any recognition that things are not so good for Edward, ask: **What can we do about it?**
6. **Listen to suggestions** – or make some yourself. Reinforce any positive responses.
7. Explain that you will be **talking to other students** about how the situation can be improved.
8. End on a positive note, but **arrange for another meeting at a definite time** to see how things have progressed.

After each student has been seen, the person who played that part can act as a **passive observer** for the next interview, in no way influencing the process.

Instructions for group member A

You are the ringleader of the group. The others seem to look up to you and are probably afraid of you. You are regarded as a tough kid who knows how to get his or her own way.

You have known the target, Edward, for several years, since primary school. He used to be a friend of yours, but you began to see him as being rather sneaky. You suspected that he was saying behind your back that you weren't as tough as you thought you were. Some others in your group also began to dislike him because he was being sarcastic at their expense.

You have orchestrated the bullying. You have encouraged your mates to gang up on Edward, to ridicule him, push him around and even send him insulting text messages.

But it does occur to you at times that maybe they are going too far. Edward has been looking very down, and **at times you feel rather sorry for him**.

One day a teacher you do not know comes into your class and asks to see you in private. You go along, without knowing what it is about.

Instructions for group member B

You are a good-natured kid and everybody seems to like you. You are good at listening to people. Being part of the group is a lot of fun. Right now everyone is having fun at Edward's expense. Nothing serious, just sort of teasing really. You are happy to join in.

True, he has looked fed up at times, but you understand that he has been nasty to some members of the group – and probably deserves what he is getting. Personally, you have nothing against him.

One day a teacher you do not know comes into your class and asks to see you in private. You go along, without knowing what it is about.

Instructions for group member C

You have been a member of a friendship group for a long time now. You have mostly enjoyed being in this group.

There is one boy called Edward who used to be a mate of yours, but he is no longer a group member. A little while ago your leader decided that everyone should start giving Edward a really hard time by mocking him and pushing him around and even sending him insulting text messages.

You went along with all this, although you did not want to. The fact is **you are scared of your group leader**, and you don't want to lose the leader's support. You think it really is unfair on Edward. But going along is the safest thing to do.

One day a teacher you do not know comes into your class and asks to see you in private. You go along, without knowing what it is about.

Role play 3: The practitioner and the targeted student

Instructions for the practitioner

You are now going to meet Edward, a student who has been bullied by a group of students.

First, explain who you are and why you have asked to see him. You can mention:

- that your role in the school is to help students to be safe, and
- that you have heard that he, Edward, has been having a hard time recently with some other students.

Ask if he would like to talk about it. Listen sympathetically and try to establish a supportive relationship.

Tell Edward that you have already talked with some students who have been giving him a hard time, and they have agreed to help. Stress that no-one is being threatened with punishment.

Gently introduce the possibility that Edward may have been doing something that led to them treating him badly. You can soften it by saying that *they* might think Edward deserves to be treated harshly, *without* suggesting that *you* might also think so.

Ask Edward to observe whether their behaviour has changed in any way.

Explain that you will be meeting with him again soon.

Instructions for the target

You, Edward, have been the victim of several weeks of very unpleasant treatment from the group you used to be friendly with. You feel both miserable and angry.

You feel you do not deserve to be treated in this way.

You recognise that at times **you might have been a bit rude yourself to some of them and maybe said a few things about one or two of them that were not very nice**. But everybody does things like that, and there was no need for them to get so nasty, for instance by sending you nasty text messages and continually making fun of you.

You would still like to be friends again with them – even though they have behaved so badly – but it doesn't seem possible.

You are prepared to talk to the practitioner about what has happened, but worried that the bullies might be punished and that things might be made worse for you.

Role play 4: The practitioner and a group of suspected bullies

Instructions for the practitioner

You meet with the three suspected bullies in a group.

Assume that you have met each one of them a second time and discovered that they have been trying to help to improve the situation with Edward.

- Begin by thanking them personally for what they have done to help improve the situation for Edward, and ask them what could be done next. They will suggest that Edward joins the group at the next meeting so they can talk to him. Agree to that.
- Explain that they will need to *plan* carefully what is to be said to him. This will take the form of a proposal.
- Give them some time in the meeting to think and talk about what they might say to Edward. Listen to their suggestions. Once a plan has been formulated get one of them to write it down.
- Have the proposal read out by the person chosen by the group to present it, and obtain everybody's agreement about what is to be said on behalf of the group when Edward joins them.
- Before ending the meeting, ask each of them to be prepared personally to say something positive – and sincere (no sarcasm) – briefly when Edward joins the group.
- Close the meeting by thanking them and explaining that Edward will be invited to the next meeting.

Instructions for each of the group members

- You have actually done something, as promised, to make things better for the target. (Be prepared, if asked, to say *what* you have done.)
- If no-one else does so, suggest that Edward be invited to join the group at the next meeting to work something out.
- Be prepared to work on a plan or proposal with other members of the group that will be made to Edward at the next meeting.
- Note the plan must be realistic and will involve a resolution not to continue the bullying, but *may* require some change in Edward's behaviour.
- You will be asked to decide on who is to be the spokesperson when the proposal is made to Edward.

Role play 5: The summit meeting – The practitioner and a group of suspected bullies plus the target

Instructions for the practitioner

You will be meeting with the three suspected bullies as a group again. Talk with them for a short while before Edward joins you.

Before Edward arrives:

- Welcome each of them by name.
- Remind them of what they have agreed to do when Edward joins the meeting; that is, say something positive about Edward, and present a proposal to Edward through a spokesperson to help bring about a solution to the problem.

When Edward arrives:

- Welcome Edward. (Seat him next to you.)
- Invite each of the suspected bullies to say something personal to Edward (as prepared).
- Ask their spokesperson to make the agreed proposal.
- Ask Edward to respond.
- Facilitate any further discussion leading to consensus.
- Raise the question of what might be done to ensure that the bullying does not start all over again. Explore options with them.
- Thank everyone and offer to help if there is any future problem.

Instructions for the group of students who met earlier with the practitioner

- Remember to act in a respectful manner throughout.
- Make sure that you have a positive thing to say to Edward at the start of the meeting – and say it when the practitioner asks you to do so.
- Be prepared to react to what Edward says *after* the proposal has been made. Some reaction or discussion is needed at this point.
- Try to reach an agreed solution to the problem that satisfies both you and Edward.

Instructions for the targeted student

- Bear in mind that you still feel aggrieved at having been treated badly by the others.
- Nevertheless you want the bullying to end.
- If it is at all possible you would like to be part of the group again.
- You will be listening to a proposal made by a group member. Respond to it as you think your character would.

Appendix 3 The Handling Bullying Questionnaire

Teachers have various ways of dealing with incidents of bullying in a school.

To some extent, what is done depends on the circumstances in which the bullying takes place, and its severity. It is, of course, sometimes difficult to generalise, but in answering the following questions, indicate what you think you might do.

Imagine the following scenario:

> A 12-year-old student is being repeatedly teased and called unpleasant names by a more powerful student who has successfully persuaded other students to avoid the targeted person as much as possible. The victim of this behaviour is feeling angry, miserable, and often isolated.

Please tick the answer which is closest to what you think you would do.

		definitely	probably	unsure	probably not	definitely not
1	I would insist that the bully 'cut it out'.					
2	I would treat the matter lightly.					
3	I would make sure the bully was suitably punished.					
4	I would discuss the matter with my colleagues at school.					
		definitely	probably	unsure	probably not	definitely not
5	I would convene a meeting of students, including the bully or bullies, tell them what was happening, and ask them to suggest ways they could help improve the situation.					
6	I would tell the victim to stand up to the bully.					
7	I would make it clear to the bully that his or her behaviour would not be tolerated.					
8	I would leave it for someone else to sort out.					
9	I would share my concern with the bully about what happened to the victim, and seek to get the bully to behave in a more caring and responsible manner.					
10	I would let the students sort it out themselves.					
11	I would suggest that the victim act more assertively.					

12	I would discuss with the bully options from which he or she could make a choice in order to improve the situation.					
13	I would ask the school counsellor to intervene.					
14	I would refer the matter to an administrator (eg principal, vice-principal, dean).					
		definitely	probably	unsure	probably not	definitely not
15	I would contact the victim's parents or guardians to express my concern about their child's wellbeing.					
16	I would just tell the kids to 'grow up'.					
17	I would encourage the victim to show that he or she could not be intimidated.					
18	I would ignore it.					
19	I would help the bully achieve greater self-esteem so that he or she would no longer want to bully anyone.					
20	I would insist to the parents or guardians of the bully that the behaviour must stop.					
21	I would find the bully something more interesting to do.					
22	I would advise the victim to tell the bully to 'back off'.					

Note: Feel free to make copies to use at your school with staff members. Afterwards you may find it useful to discuss why members answered as they did.

Appendix 4 A suggested timeline for applying the Method of Shared Concern

Day 1	Successive meetings with individual suspected bullies	SB1
		SB2
		SB3
Day 2	Meeting with target	T
Day 3	No meetings	
Day 4	Further brief meetings with individual suspected bullies	SB1
		SB2
		SB3
Day 5	Follow up meetings if necessary	
Day 6	Group meeting* of suspected bullies	SB1+SB2+SB3
Day 7	Second meeting with target	T
Day 8	Summit meeting with suspected bullies and target	SB1+SB2+SB3+T

*This can only be held when progress has already been demonstrated through actions undertaken, and confirmed by the practitioner.

Appendix 5 Test questions on the Method of Shared Concern

Circle your answer.

1. It is considered best to gather information about the bullying initially from:
   (a) parents
   (b) the target of the bullying
   (c) people who have been told about it or seen it happening
   (d) friends of the suspected bullies

2. In selecting the first suspected bully to interview:
   (a) start with the suspected ringleader
   (b) choose the person who seems to have been the least involved in the bullying
   (c) pick at random
   (d) consult with teachers

3. In interviewing each suspected bully:
   (a) begin by asking what he or she knows about the bullying
   (b) express concern regarding the target's situation
   (c) ask the suspected bully whether he or she is enjoying life at school
   (d) inquire as to whether the suspected bully is at all concerned about the current plight of the victim

4. Once the suspected bully has acknowledged that the victim's situation is not so good:
   (a) ask what can be done to improve the situation
   (b) explore why the suspected bully believes that this is so
   (c) ask the suspected bully how he or she would feel in the victim's situation
   (d) make it clear that everyone has a responsibility to help the victim

5. If the suspected bully appears reluctant to acknowledge that the target is having a hard time:
   (a) suggest that he or she knows more about the situation than he or she is prepared to admit
   (b) try a new tack; for example, ask how the suspected bully and friends generally spend their leisure time together, then come back to the victim's predicament
   (c) terminate the interview immediately
   (d) tell the suspected bully that you will be getting in touch with his or her parents.

6. In the course of the interview:
   (a) indicate that it is quite understandable that the suspected bully would sometimes engage in bullying the 'victim'
   (b) avoid blaming the suspected bully for any action he or she has taken
   (c) agree with everything the suspected bully says
   (d) suggest that the suspected bully may personally be afraid of being bullied by a member of his or her group.

7. Before interviewing the suspected bully:
   (a) obtain parent or guardian permission to do so
   (b) make sure there is good evidence that the suspected bully is actually guilty of the bullying offence
   (c) talk over the matter with the victim
   (d) do none of the above.

8. Before concluding the interview:
   (a) thank the suspected bully for any positive suggestions he or she has made about how the victim can be helped.
   (b) explain that the suspected bully may or may not be interviewed again at a later stage
   (c) indicate that the suspected bully would be letting you down if his or her promises are not honoured
   (d) mention that you are now going on to talk to the victim.

9. When you meet with the victim, which of the following should not be done?
   (a) Listen sympathetically to the victim's account of events.
   (b) Explore the possibility that he/she could in some way have provoked the bullying.
   (c) Share with the victim that you have been talking with some students who have been involved in the bullying.
   (d) Assure the victim that you have spoken to the bullies and the problem has been solved.

10. Before convening a group meeting with the suspected bullies only:
    (a) check out with individuals whether progress has been made towards resolving the problem
    (b) get the permission of the victim before the meeting is held
    (c) assume that the suspected bullies have all honoured their promises
    (d) inform the parents of each of the suspected bullies before the meeting is held.

11. Convening a meeting with the group of suspected bullies:
    (a) is unnecessary if good progress has already been made with individual suspected bullies
    (b) can occur when the practitioner is confident that the suspected bullies have already taken steps to improve the situation for the victim
    (c) requires the permission of the target before the meeting can go ahead
    (d) can include some other students who are expected to encourage the suspected bullies to act constructively.

12. In conducting the meeting with the group of suspected bullies only:
    (a) indicate that you are pleased about the progress that has been made towards resolving the problem
    (b) ask them to reflect on what they were thinking about in causing harm to one of their peers
    (c) tell them that they must now collectively meet with the victim and say how sorry they are to have upset him or her
    (d) explain to them that they are free *not* to attend the next meeting if they so wish.

13. In preparing the group for the next meeting which of the following would the practitioner **not** do:
    (a) require that they make a plan or proposal to put to the victim on how they hope to resolve the problem
    (b) ask them to be prepared to say something positive to the victim when he or she joins them
    (c) remind them that the target has been offended against and is in no way responsible for what has ensued
    (d) be prepared to listen to what the target has to say when suggestions are made about how the problem might be resolved.

14. Prior to the meeting of the suspected bullies with the victim:
    (a) meet with the target and invite him or her to come to the meeting
    (b) insist that the target comes to the meeting
    (c) make it clear that the suspected bullies will be apologising for what they have done
    (d) invite other interested students to join them at the meeting.

15. During the meeting of the suspected bullies with the target:
    (a) begin by asking the target to speak up about how hurt or upset he or she has felt as a result of the bad treatment received
    (b) have the bullies individually apologise for what they have done
    (c) allow negotiations to take place that might result in everyone agreeing to adjust their behaviour towards each other
    (d) insist that the target on no account should bear any responsibility for what has happened.

16. If during the meeting anyone makes a statement that you know is untrue:
    (a) confront the speaker with contrary evidence
    (b) just agree with the speaker's version of what happened
    (c) require that the speaker clearly justifies what has been said
    (d) seek to move the discussion on so as to focus on what could help improve the situation.

17. If it becomes clear that there are differences of opinion as to how the problem should be resolved:
    (a) play a passive role, and let them sort out any differences without making any suggestions
    (b) seek to arbitrate; ask them to agree with your considered judgement on what needs to be done
    (c) act the part of the mediator between the suspected bullies and the target
    (d) insist that everybody signs a contract at the conclusion of the meeting stating how they have agreed to behave towards each other.

18. Shared Concern is considered to be **most** appropriate:
    (a) in cases of low level bullying or teasing
    (b) when bullying is exceptionally severe
    (c) in cases of moderate severity when a group of students is involved as perpetrators
    (d) with students of all ages.

19. Regarding the Method of Shared Concern:
    (a) it is a theoretical procedure for which there is only anecdotal evidence regarding its effectiveness
    (b) so far there has been no research evidence in support of the method
    (c) male practitioners should always work with boys; female practitioners with girls
    (d) the method has been assessed as to its effectiveness in several countries and has been shown to achieve a high measure of success.

20. The Method of Shared Concern assumes that:
    (a) bullies are unaware of the hurt they cause
    (b) bullies are typically under the influence of the group to which they belong
    (c) bullies are highly aggressive individuals with psychotic tendencies
    (d) bullies are lacking in normal empathic feeling.

21. According to the Method of Shared Concern, which one is **untrue**?
    (a) Bullies are sometimes afraid of being bullied by other group members.
    (b) Victims may sometimes act provocatively and bring on the bullying.
    (c) Punishment of schoolchildren can never be justified – not even when bullying involves serious criminal action.
    (d) Bullies are not responsible for the harm they do.

22. In applying Shared Concern:
    (a) it is considered acceptable for more than one practitioner or teacher to be present during the interviews
    (b) an important aim of the method is to re-individualise students who are being unduly controlled in a negative way by the group to which they belong
    (c) under no circumstances must the method be abandoned once it has begun
    (d) there is an assumption that schools should **not** have rules or guidelines about how children should behave.

Answers

The answers given below are consistent with what has been indicated *in this book*. Schools may, of course, decide that the method should be used in a different way, for example by requiring parent approval before interviewing students.

The proposed answers

1. It is considered best to gather information about the bullying initially from **(c) people who have been told about it or seen it happening.**
2. In selecting the first suspected bully to interview, **(a) start with the suspected ringleader.**
3. In interviewing each suspected bully, **(b) express concern regarding the target's situation.**
4. Once the suspected bully has acknowledged that the victim's situation is not so good, **(a) ask what can be done to improve the situation.**
5. If the suspected bully appears reluctant to acknowledge that the target is having a hard time, **(b) try a new tack; for example, ask how the suspected bully and friends generally spend their leisure time together, then come back to the victim's predicament.**
6. In the course of the interview, **(b) avoid blaming the suspected bully for any action he or she has taken.**
7. Before interviewing the suspected bully, **(d) do none of the above.**
8. Before concluding the interview, **(a) thank the suspected bully for any positive suggestions he/she has made about how the victim can be helped.**
9. When you meet with the victim which of the following should not be done? **(d) Assure the victim that you have spoken to the bullies and the problem has been solved.**
10. Before convening a group meeting with the suspected bullies only, **(a) check out with individuals whether progress has been made towards resolving the problem.**
11. Convening a meeting with the suspected bullies **(b) can occur when the practitioner is confident that the suspected bullies have already taken steps to improve the situation for the victim.**

12. In conducting the meeting with the group of suspected bullies only, **(a) indicate that you are pleased about the progress that has been made towards resolving the problem.**
13. In preparing the group for the next meeting, which of the following would the practitioner not do? **(c) Remind them that the target has been offended against and is in no way responsible for what has ensued.**
14. Prior to the meeting of the suspected bullies with the victim, **(a) meet with the target and invite him or her to come to the meeting.**
15. During the meeting of the suspected bullies with the target, **(c) allow negotiations to take place that might result in everyone agreeing to adjust their behaviour towards each other.**
16. If during the meeting anyone makes a statement that you know is untrue, **(d) seek to move the discussion on so as to focus on what could help improve the situation.**
17. If it becomes clear that there are differences of opinion as to how the problem should be resolved, **(c) act the part of the mediator between the suspected bullies and the target.**
18. Shared Concern is considered to be most appropriate **(c) in cases of moderate severity when a group of students is involved as perpetrators.**
19. Regarding the Method of Shared Concern, **(d) the method has been assessed as to its effectiveness in several countries and has been shown to achieve a high measure of success.**
20. The Method of Shared Concern assumes that **(b) bullies are typically under the influence of the group to which they belong.**
21. According to the Method of Shared Concern, which one is untrue? **(d) Bullies are not responsible for the harm they do.**
22. In applying Shared Concern, **(b) an important aim of the method is to re-individualise students who are being unduly controlled in a negative way by the group to which they belong.**

Appendix 6 Training resources

Background reading

Beaulieu, A.B., & Rousseau, N. (2004). *La méthode dintérêt commun (mic): Intervenir stratégiquement auprès des intimidateurs et de leurs victims par Anatol Pikas.* Service régional de soutien et d'expertise en troubles du comportement et psychopathologie en Montérégie.

Griffiths, C. (2001). *Countering bullying in schools training package.* Perth: Western Australian Department of Education.

Griffiths, C., & Weatherilt, T. (2008). *Pikas' Shared Concern method (SCm) staff skills training package.* Perth: Department of Education and Training.

Pikas, A. (1989). A pure concept of mobbing gives the best results for treatment. *School Psychology International,* 10, 95–104.

Pikas, A. (1989). The common concern method for the treatment of mobbing. In E. Roland & E. Munthe (Eds.), *Bullying: An international perspective.* London: Fulton.

Pikas, A. (2002). New developments of the Shared Concern method. *School Psychology International,* 23(3), 307–336.

Rigby, K. (2007). The Method of Shared Concern as an intervention technique to address bullying in schools: An overview and appraisal, *Australian Journal of Counselling and Guidance,* 15, 27–34.

Rigby, K. (2010). Breaking the cycle. *Education Review,* March, 8–9.

Rigby, K. (2010). *Bullying interventions in schools: Six basic approaches.* Melbourne: ACER.

Rigby, K. (2010). School bullying and the case for the Method of Shared Concern. In S. Jimerson, S. Swearer & D. Espelage (Eds.), *The handbook of school bullying: An international perspective.* New York: Routledge, pp. 547–558.

Rigby, K & Griffiths, C. (2010). *Applying the Method of Shared Concern in Australian schools: An evaluative study.* Canberra: Department of Education, Employment and Workplace Relations. Download at <http://www.deewr.gov.au/Schooling/NationalSafeSchools/Documents/covertBullyReports/MethodOFSharedConcern.pdf>.

Rigby, K. & Griffiths, C. (2011, in press). The Method of Shared Concern, *School Psychology International.*

Rigby, K. & Thomas, E.B. (2010). *How schools counter bullying: policies and procedures in selected Australian schools* (revised edition). Melbourne: ACER.

DVDs and vodcasts

Readymade Productions (2007). *The Method of Shared Concern: a staff training resource for dealing with bullying in schools,* Adelaide, Readymade Productions. Access at <http://www.readymade.com.au/method>.

Rigby, K. (2007). *Bullying in schools: six methods of intervention.* Loggerhead Productions. This DVD contains a representation of the Method of Shared Concern in the context of five other approaches. Download clips from DVD at <http://www.loggerheadfilms.co.uk/products-page/?category=1&product_id=4>. The DVD is obtainable from ACER, Camberwell, Victoria. ph: 1800 338 402, +61 3 9277 5447.

Rigby, K. (2007). *Bullying and harassment: Six vodcasts.* Education Queensland. http://education.qld.gov.au/studentservices/protection/community/bullying.html (This series includes a discussion of the Method of Shared Concern.

Advisers and trainers

Like most intervention methods, the Method of Shared Concern is best understood and applied by working with those who have gained practical experience in its application. Here is a list of educators whose background knowledge and experience is such that they are able to help those who are interested in using the method. Each of them is prepared to give advice and, where practicable, to offer workshops.

Australia

New South Wales

Ms Nicki Tunica
Deputy principal, Jamison High School
222 Evan St, Penrith, NSW 2750
phone: 02 4731 6150
email: nicolette.tunica@det.nsw.edu.au

Ms Deborah Henderson
Principal, Wentworthville Public School
cnr Station St & Fullagar Rd, Wentworthville, NSW 2145
phone: 02 9631 8529; fax 02 9896 3079
email:deborah.henderson@det.nsw.edu.au

South Australia

Mr Bill Bates
South Australian Police Force
mobile: 0403 337 772
email: eandb@adam.com.au

Ms Kerry Jarvis
Education sector
mobile: 0419 922 669
email: kjarvis@adam.com.au

Professor Ken Rigby
School of Education
University of South Australia
phone: 08 8302 1371
mobile: 0410 035 500
website: www.kenrigby.net

Ms Meg Collins
School counsellor
PO Box 177 Uraidla, SA 5142
phone: 08 8337 6844
mobile: 0423 020 998 or 0423 020 998
email: meg.collins@charlescss.sa.edu.au or gemcol@bigpond.com

Tasmania

Ms Angela Gatti
Counsellor, student support
Deloraine High School
email: angela.gatti@education.tas.gov.au

Victoria

Ms Sue Renn
Grampians Regional Office, Ballarat
Department of Education & Early Childhood Development
109 Armstrong St, Ballarat, Vic 3350
phone: 03 5337 8402
email: renn.susan.l@edumail.vic.gov.au

Ms Jacqueline Van Velsen
Education officer, youth services
Catholic Education Office, Ballarat
PO Box 576, Ballarat, Vic 3353
phone: 03 5337 7135
fax: 03 5331 5166
mobile: 0407 523 780
website: www.ceo.balrt.catholic.edu.au

Western Australia

Ms Coosje Griffiths
Area manager, student services
Swan Education District
Department of Education
18 Blackboy Way, Beechboro, WA 6063
phone: 08 9442 6637
mobile: 040 9085 973

Mr Len Barrett
School counsellor, Mercy College
cnr Beach Rd & Mirrabooka Ave, Koondoola
(PO Box 42 Mirrabooka) WA 6941
phone: 08 9247 9242
fax: 08 9247 9296
email: barrett.len@mercy.wa.edu.au

Mr Andrew Olson
Senior psychologist
West Coast Education District
Department of Education
phone: 08 9406 7300
fax: 08 9406 7311
mobile: 0403 539 174
email: olyandrew@gmail.com

Canada

Ms Eva de Gosztonyi
Coordinator
Centre of Excellence for Behaviour Management
Riverside School Board
299 Sir Wilfrid Laurier St, Lambert, QC, Canada, J4R 2V7
phone: +1 450 672 4010 ext. 6066
mobile: +1 514 771 4649
email: edegosztonyi@rsb.qc.ca

England

Professor Peter Smith
Head, Unit for School and Family Studies
Department of Psychology
Goldsmiths, University of London
New Cross, SE14 6NW, United Kingdom
phone: +44 20 7919 7898
fax: +44 20 7919 7873
email: p.smith@gold.ac.uk

Dr Sonia Sharp
Executive Director
Children and Young People's Service
Sheffield City Council
Town Hall, Pinstone Street, Sheffield,
South Yorkshire, S1 2HH, United Kingdom
phone: +44 0114 273 5726
fax: +44 0114 273 5652
email: sonia.sharp@sheffield.gov.uk

Estonia

Ms Merit Lage, Tallinn, Estonia
email: merit@lastekaitseliit.ee

Finland

Professor Christina Salmivalli
University of Turku, Finland
phone: +358 2 333 5426,
fax: +358 2 333 5060
mobile: +358 400 995 473;
websites: www.kivakoulu.fi, www.gspsy.fi

Germany

Mr Bernhard Meissner (Würzburg, Germany)
Director, European Training Centre
International School Psychology Association (ISPA)
Phone: +49-931-04629
Email: meissner@ispaweb.org
website:www.ispaweb.org

Ireland

Professor Keith Sullivan
School of Education
National University of Ireland, Galway
University Road, Galway, Ireland.,
telephone: +353 91 492158
email: Keith.Sullivan@nuigalway.ie

New Zealand

Mr Adam Heath
Middle School principal, Kristin School
phone: +64 9 415 9566 ext. 2319
website: www.kristin.school.nz

Spain

Professor Rosario Ortega
Head, Department of Psychology
University of Cordoba
San Alberto Magno S/N, 14004 Cordoba, Spain
phone: +34 957 212 601
mobile: +34 618 579 962

Sweden

Dr Anatol Pikas
email: anatol@pikas.se

Ms Marie Liljenbrand-Skog
email: marie.liljenbrand-skoog@orebro.se

Ms Malin Sundström
email: malin.sundstrom@umea.se

United States

Associate Professor Sheri Bauman
Director
School Counseling Program
College of Education
University of Arizona
PO Box 210069, Tucson, AZ, 85721-0069, USA
phone: +1 520 626 7308,
email: sherib@u.arizona.edu

References

Allport, F. H. (1924). *Social psychology*. Boston: Houghton Mifflin.

Baldry, A. C., & Farrington, D. P. (2000). Bullies and delinquents: Personal characteristics and parental styles. *Journal of Community and Applied Social Psychology*, 10(1), 17–31.

Ball, H. A., Arseneault, A., Taylor, A., Maughan, B., Caspi, A., & Moffitt, T. E. (2008). Genetic and environmental influences on victims, bullies and bully–victims in childhood. *Journal of Child Psychology and Psychiatry*, 49(1), 104–112.

Bauer, N. S., Lozano, P., & Rivara, F. P. (2007). The effectiveness of the Olweus Bullying Prevention Program in public middle schools: A controlled trial. *Journal of Adolescent Health*, 40(3), 266–274.

Bauman, S. (2011). *Cyberbullying: What counselors need to know*. Alexandria, VA: American Counseling Association.

Bauman, S., & Del Rio, A. (2005). Knowledge and beliefs about bullying in schools. School *Psychology International*, 26(4), 428–442.

Bauman, S., Rigby, K., & Hoppa, K. (2008). US teachers' and school counsellors' strategies for handling school bullying incidents. *Educational Psychology*, 28(7), 837–856. <http://pdfserve.informaworld.com/931527_731196606_903076702.pdf>.

Beaulieu, A. B., & Rousseau, N. (2004). *La méthode dintérêt commun (mic): intervenir stratégiquement auprès des intimidateurs et de leurs victims par Anatol Pikas*. Service régional de soutien et d'expertise en troubles du comportement et psychopathologie en Montérégie.

Bellhouse, B. (2009). *Beginner's guide to circle time with primary school students*. Sydney: Inyahead Press.

Berlan, E. D., Corliss, H. L., Field, A. E., Goodman, E., & Austin, S. (2010). Sexual orientation and bullying among adolescents in the Growing Up Today study. *Journal of Adolescent Health*, 46(4), 366–371.

Blake, E., Rigby, K., & Johnson, B. (2004). Bullying and the bystander: Behaviour at school. *Principal Matters*, August, 2–3.

Bretall, R. (Ed.). (1973). *A Kierkegaard anthology*. Princeton: Princeton Paperback Editions, pp. 333–334. Quotations from S. Kierkegaard (1848). 'The point of view for my work as an author'.

Chan, J. H. F. (2006). Systemic patterns in bullying and victimization. *School Psychology International*, 27(3), 352–369.

Cowie, H., Smith, P. K., Boulton, M. & Laver, R. (1994). *Cooperation in the multi-ethnic classroom*. London: David Fulton.

Cowie, H., & Wallace, P. (2000). *Peer support in action: From bystanding to standing by.* London: Sage.

Cremin, H. (2008). *Peer mediation: Citizenship and social inclusion revisited.* New York: Open University.

Duncan, A. (1996). The Shared Concern method for resolving group bullying in schools. *Educational Psychology in Practice,* 12, 94–98.

Egan, S. K., & Perry, D. G. (1998). Does low self-regard invite victimization? *Developmental Psychology,* 34(2), 299–309.

Festinger, L. (1957). *A theory of cognitive dissonance.* Stanford, CA: Stanford University Press.

Findley, I. (2006). *Shared responsibility: Beating bullying in Australian schools.* Melbourne: ACER Press.

Griffiths, C. (2001). *Countering bullying in schools training package.* Perth: Western Australian Department of Education.

Griffiths, C & Weatherilt, T. (2008). *Pikas' Shared Concern method (SCm) staff skills training package.* Perth: Department of Education and Training.

Jimerson, S., Swearer, S. & Espelage, D. (Eds.). (2009). *Handbook of bullying in schools: An international perspective.* New York: Routledge.

Jolliffe, D., & Farrington, D. P. (2006). Examining the relationship between low empathy and bullying. *Aggressive Behavior,* 32, 540–550.

Jung, C. G. (1981, 2nd Edition). *The archetypes and the collective unconscious.* In *Collected Works,* Vol. 9, Pt. 1, Princeton, NJ: Bollingen.

Kaukiainen, A., Björkqvist, K., Lagerspetz, K., Österman, K., Salmivalli, C., Forsblom, S. et al. (1999). The relationships between social intelligence, empathy, and three types of aggression. *Aggressive Behaviour,* 25, 81–89.

Koestler, A. (1967). *The ghost in the machine.* London: Macmillan.

Le Bon, G. (1895). *The crowd: A study of the popular mind.* See <http://www.gutenberg.org/dirs/etext96/tcrwd10.txt>.

McLoughlin, C. S. (2009). Positive peer group interventions: An alternative to individualized interventions for promoting prosocial behavior in potentially disaffected youth. *Electronic Journal of Research in Educational Psychology,* 7, 1131–1156.

Molcho, M., Craig, W., Due, P., Pickett, W., Harel-Fisch, Y., Overpeck, M. et al. (2009). Cross-national time trends in bullying behaviour 1994–2006: Findings from Europe and North America. *International Journal of Public Health,* 54, 225–234.

Murdoch, W. (1947). *72 Essays: A selection.* London: Angus & Robertson.

Nansel, T. R., Craig, W., Overpeck, M. D., Saluja, G., Ruan, W. J., & Health Behaviour in School-aged Children Bullying Analyses Working Group (2004). Cross-national consistency in the relationship between bullying behaviors and psychosocial adjustment. *Archives of Pediatric and Adolescent Medicine,* 158, 730–736.

Nansel, T. R., Overpeck, M., Pilla, R. S., Ruan, W. J., Simons-Morton, B., & Scheidt, P. (2001). Bullying behaviors among US youth: Prevalence and association with psychosocial adjustment. *Journal of the American Medical Association*, 2094–2100.

Nettelbeck, T., & Wilson, C. (2002). Personal vulnerability to victimization of people with mental retardation. *Trauma, Violence, and Abuse*, 3, 289–306.

Neufeld, G. & Mate, G. (2004). *Hold on to your kids: Why parents need to matter more than peers.* Toronto: Vintage.

Olweus, D. (1993). *Bullying at school.* Oxford & Cambridge, MA: Blackwell Publishers.

Olweus, D., Limber, S. P., & Mihalic, S. (1999). *The bullying prevention program: Blueprints for violence prevention*, Vol. 10. Boulder, CO: Center for the Study and Prevention of Violence.

Ortega, R., Del Rey, R., & Mora-Merchan, J. A. (2004). SAVE model: An antibullying intervention in Spain. In P. K. Smith, D. Pepler, & K. Rigby (Eds.), *Bullying in schools: How successful can interventions be?* Cambridge: Cambridge University Press, pp. 167–186.

Pepler, D. J. & Craig, W. M. (1995). A peek behind the fence: Naturalistic observations of aggressive children with remote audiovisual recording. *Developmental Psychology*, 31, 545–553.

Petersen, L. & Rigby, K. (1999). Countering bullying at an Australian secondary school. *Journal of Adolescence*, 22(4), 481–492.

Pikas, A. (1989a). A pure concept of mobbing gives the best results for treatment. School *Psychology International*, 10, 95–104.

Pikas, A. (1989b). The common concern method for the treatment of mobbing. In E. Roland & E. Munthe (Eds.), *Bullying: An international perspective.* London: Fulton.

Pikas, A. (2002). New developments of the Shared Concern method. School *Psychology International*, 23(3), 307–336.

Readymade Productions (2007). *The Method of Shared Concern: A staff training resource for dealing with bullying in schools.* Adelaide: Readymade Productions, <http//www.readymade.com.au/method>.

Rigby, K. (1993). School children's perceptions of their families and parents as a function of peer relations. *Journal of Genetic Psychology*, 154(4), 501–514.

Rigby, K. (1998a). *Manual for the Peer Relations Questionnaire* (PRQ). Point Lonsdale, Victoria: The Professional Reading Guide.

Rigby, K. (1998b). The relationship between reported health and involvement in bully/victim problems among male and female secondary school students. *Journal of Health Psychology*, 3(4), 465–476.

Rigby, K. (1999). Peer victimisation at school and the health of secondary students. *British Journal of Educational Psychology*, 22(2), 28–34.

Rigby, K. (2001). Health consequences of bullying and its prevention in schools. In J. Juvonen & S. Graham (Eds.), *Peer harassment in school.* New York: Guilford.

Rigby, K. (2002). *New perspectives on bullying.* London: Jessica Kingsley.

Rigby, K. (2003). Consequences of bullying in schools. *The Canadian Journal of Psychiatry*, 48, 583–590.

Rigby, K. (2005). The Method of Shared Concern as an intervention technique to address bullying in schools: An overview and appraisal. *Australian Journal of Counselling and Guidance*, 15, 27–34.

Rigby, K. (2006). Implications of bullying for aggression between nations. *Journal of Peace Education*, 175–186.

Rigby, K. (2008). *Children and bullying: How parents and educators can reduce bullying at school.* Malden: Blackwell/Wiley.

Rigby, K. (2009a). *Bullying and harassment: Six vodcasts*. Education Queensland. See <http://education.qld.gov.au/studentservices/protection/community/bullying.html>.

Rigby, K. (2009b). *Bullying in schools: Six methods of intervention*. Loggerhead Productions. Download clips from DVD at <http://www.loggerheadfilms.co.uk/products-page/?category=1&product_id=4>. The DVD is obtainable from ACER (www.acerpress.com.au).

Rigby, K. (2010a). Breaking the cycle. *Education Review*, March, 8–9.

Rigby, K. (2010b). *Bullying interventions in schools: Six basic approaches*. Melbourne: ACER.

Rigby, K. (2010c). School bullying and the case for the Method of Shared Concern. In S. Jimerson, S. Swearer & D. Espelage (Eds.), *Handbook of bullying in schools: An international perspective*. New York: Routledge, pp. 547–558.

Rigby, K. (2010d). *The Peer Relations Assessment Questionnaires*. Melbourne: ACER.

Rigby, K. & Bagshaw, D. (2003). Prospects of adolescent students collaborating with teachers in addressing issues of bullying and conflict in schools. *Educational Psychology*, 32, 535–546.

Rigby, K., & Barnes, A. (2002). To tell or not to tell: The victimised student's dilemma. *Youth Studies Australia*, 21(3), 33–36.

Rigby, K. & Bauman, S. (2007). What teachers think should be done about cases of bullying. *Professional Educator*, 6, pp. 9–12.

Rigby, K. & Bauman, S. (2009). How school personnel tackle cases of bullying: A critical examination. In S. Jimerson, S. Swearer & D. Espelage (Eds.), *Handbook of bullying in schools: An international perspective*. New York: Routledge, pp. 455–468.

Rigby, K., Cox, I. K. & Black, G. (1997). Cooperativeness and bully/victim problems among Australian schoolchildren. *Journal of Social Psychology*, 137(3), 357–368.

Rigby, K., & Griffiths, C. (2010). *Applying the Method of Shared Concern in Australian schools: An evaluative study*. Canberra: Department of Education, Employment and Workplace Relations. Access at <http://www.deewr.gov.au/Schooling/NationalSafeSchools/Documents/covertBullyReports/MethodOFSharedConcern.pdf>.

Rigby, K., & Griffiths, C. (2011, in press). The Method of Shared Concern. *School Psychology International*.

Rigby, K., & Johnson, B. (2006). Expressed readiness of Australian school children to act as bystanders in support of children who are being bullied. *Educational Psychology*, 26, 425–440.

Rigby, K., & Slee, P. T. (1999). Suicidal ideation among adolescent school children, involvement in bully/victim problems and perceived low social support. *Suicide and Life-threatening Behavior*, 29, 119–130.

Rigby, K., Slee, P. T., & Martin, G. (2007). Implications of inadequate parental bonding and peer victimization for adolescent mental health. *Journal of Adolescence*, 30(5), 801–812.

Rivers, R., & Noret, N. (2009). I h8 u: Findings from a five-year study of text and email bullying. *British Educational Research Journal*, 36(4), 643–671.

Robinson, G., & Maines, B. (2008). *Bullying: A complete guide to the Support Group Method*. London: Sage.

Roland, E. (2002). Bullying, depressive symptoms and suicidal thoughts. *Educational Research*, 44(1), 55–67.

Rønning, J. A., Sourander, A., Kumpulainen, K., Tamminen, T., Niemelä, S., Moilanen, I. et al. (2009). Cross-informant agreement about bullying and victimization among eight-year-olds: Whose information best predicts psychiatric caseness 10–15 years later? *Social Psychiatry and Psychiatric Epidemiology*, 44, 15–22.

Russell, B. (1938). *Power*. London: George Allen & Unwin.

Salmivalli, C., Kaukiainen, A., Voeten, M., & Sinisammal, M. (2004). Targeting the group as a whole: The Finnish anti-bullying intervention. In P. K. Smith, D. Pepler, & K. Rigby (Eds.), *Bullying in schools: How successful can interventions be?* Cambridge: Cambridge University Press, pp. 251–274.

Slee, P. T., & Rigby, K. (1993). The relationship of Eysenck's personality factors and self-esteem to bully/victim behaviour in Australian school boys. *Personality and Individual Differences*, 14, 371–373.

Smith, P. K. (1997). Bullying in life-span perspective: What can studies of school bullying and workplace bullying learn from each other? *Journal of Community and Applied Social Psychology*, 7(3), 249–255.

Smith, P. K. (2001). Should we blame the bullies? *The Psychologist*, 14(2).

Smith, P. K., Howard, S., & Thompson, F. (2007). Use of the Support Group Method to tackle bullying, and evaluation from schools and local authorities in England. *Pastoral Care in Education*, 25, 4–13.

Smith, P. K., Mahdavi, J., Carvalho, M., Fisher, S., Russell, S., & Tippett, N. (2008). Cyberbullying: Its nature and impact in secondary school pupils. *Journal of Child Psychology and Psychiatry*, 49, 376–385.

Smith, P. K. & Sharp, S. (Eds.) (1994). *School bullying: Insights and perspectives*. London: Routledge.

Smith, P. K., Sharp, S., Eslea, M., & Thompson, D. (2004). England: The Sheffield Project. In P. K. Smith, D. Pepler, & K. Rigby (Eds.), *Bullying in schools: How successful can interventions be?* Cambridge: Cambridge University Press, pp. 99–124.

Smith, P.K. & Shu, S. (2000). What good schools can do about bullying: Findings from a survey in English schools after a decade of research and action. *Childhood*, 7, 193–212.

Solberg, M. E., & Olweus, D. (2003). Prevalence estimation of school bullying with the Olweus Bully/Victim Questionnaire, *Aggressive Behavior*, 29, 239–268.

Sullivan, K. (2010). *The anti-bullying handbook* (2nd Edition). London: Sage

Sutton, J., & Keogh, E. (2001). Components of Machiavellian beliefs in children: Relationships with personality. *Personality and Individual Differences*, 30, 137–148.

Thorsborne, M., & Vinegrad, D. (2006). *Restorative practice and the management of bullying: Rethinking behaviour management*. Queenscliff, Victoria: Inyahead Press.

Troy, M., & Sroufe, L. A. (1987). Victimization among preschoolers: Role of attachment relationship history. *Journal of the American Academy of Child and Adolescent Psychiatry*, 26, 166–172.

Voss, L. D., & Mulligan, J. (2000). Bullying in schools: Are short pupils more at risk? Questionnaire study in a cohort. *British Medical Journal*, 320, 612–613.

Index

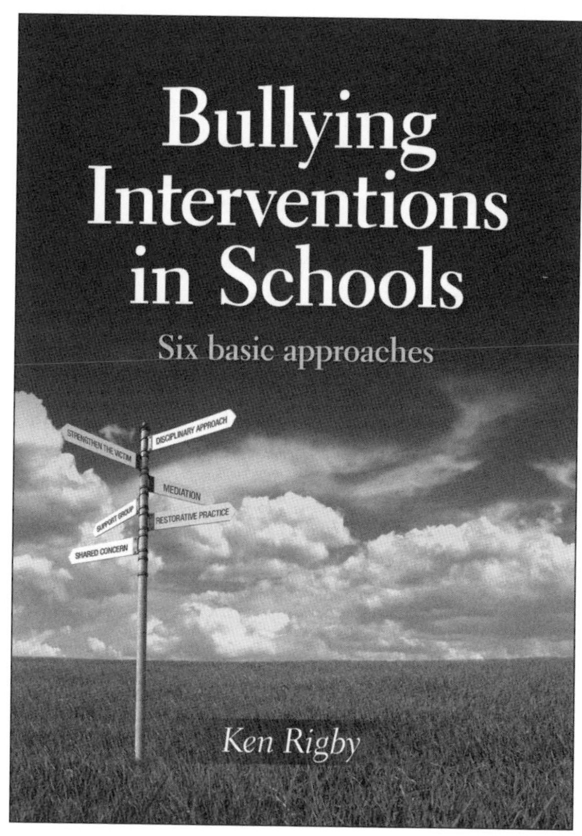

Bullying Interventions in Schools

Six basic approaches

Ken Rigby

Dealing effectively with the problem of bullying in schools is now recognised as a major challenge for educators of young people. Successful interventions to stop, or even reduce, bullying in schools are difficult to achieve; however, the case for improving the effectiveness of school interventions in cases of bullying is overwhelming.

More attention needs to be paid to what can be done in addressing actual cases of bullying, as well as seeking to create a school environment in which the task may be more manageable. Schools need to be aware of the range of approaches that may be adopted and applied in dealing with individual cases. *Bullying Interventions in Schools* examines in detail the six major intervention methods: the traditional disciplinary approach; strengthening the victim; mediation; restorative practice; the support group method; and the method of shared concern.

Bullying Interventions in Schools aims to promote an understanding of what methods exist to address actual cases of bullying, and when and how they can best be applied. Each method is described in detail, together with its rationale. In addition, the strengths and limitations of their use are critically examined, drawing upon research-based evidence regarding their efficacy and applicability for different kinds and degrees of bullying encountered in schools.

To order *Bullying Interventions in Schools: Six basic approaches*

w: http://shop.acer.edu.au

e: sales@acer.edu.au

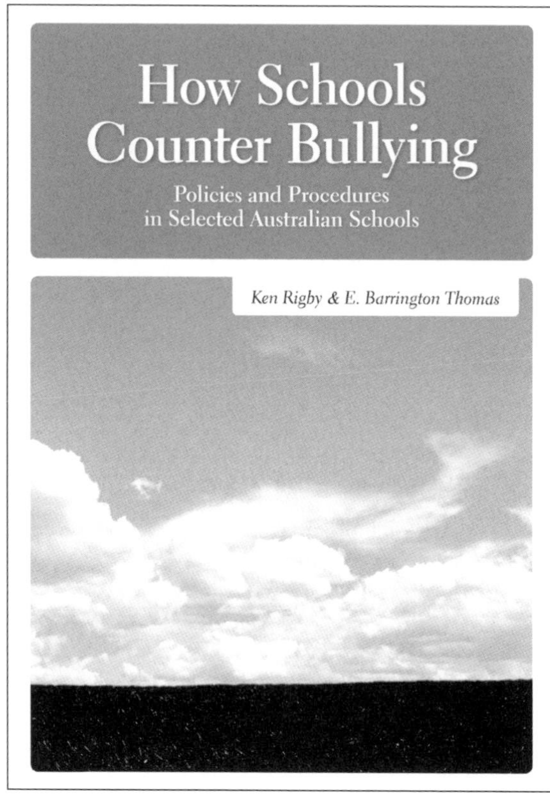

How Schools Counter Bullying

Policies and procedures in selected Australian schools

Ken Rigby and E. Barrington Thomas

This book provides the background to the research that was conducted using the *Peer Relations Assessment Questionnaire (PRAQ)* for the Criminology Research Council. The resulting qualitative and quantitative data on how schools in Australia have dealt with bullying is provided. It also describes specific policies, plans and activities that schools have been able to implement to counter bullying. The effectiveness and impact of various approaches in working with the whole school, introducing pro-social curriculum content and dealing with specific bullying incidents are also discussed. Based on the research and experience, advice and guidance is given on implementing effective anti-bullying strategies within the school.

To order *How Schools Counter Bullying: Policies and procedures in selected Australian schools*

w: http://shop.acer.edu.au

e: sales@acer.edu.au

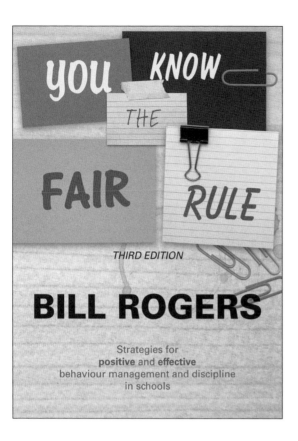